Business Organisations and Systems

CONTENTS

OUTLINE

The aim of this unit is to examine business organisations in the private (market) and public (command) sectors at both local and national levels. The unit introduces organisations in terms of the different structures, purposes, liabilities, legal constraints and obligations, and objectives. The systems that support organisations and the impact of information technology on administrative procedures are explored. The content of the unit not only develops an understanding of the functions of the business but also an appreciation of how organisations work on a day-to-day basis.

D1340466

Note: each of the Collins Educational Advanced GNVQ
Business Units have been published separately. Figures have
been numbered according to the Unit in which they appear.

Melvyn Butcher, Philip Gunn and David Collinson assert the
moral right to be identified as the authors of this work.

Published by
Collins Educational Ltd
An imprint of HarperCollins *Publishers*
77–85 Fulham Palace Road
Hammersmith
London W6 8JB

First published 1995

ISBN 0003224481

Designed and edited by DSM Partnership.
Cover designed by Trevor Burrows.
Project managed by Antonia Maxwell.
Printed and bound by Scotprint Ltd., Musselburgh, Scotland.

ACKNOWLEDGEMENTS
The authors and publisher would like to thank the following
for permission to reproduce material:

Daily Express, Sascha Olofson, 'Virtual dream for shoppers'
(p. 31)

Reuters, material from diagram 'Corporate information –
growth over ten years' (pp. 51 and 57)

Universal Press Syndicate ©, Doonesbury cartoon by Garry
Trudeau (p. 56)

Cartoonists & Writers Syndicate, cartoon by Kal (p. 58)

Computer Weekly, Karl Schneider, 'Data transfers make the
news' (p. 59)

Every effort has been made to contact copyright holders, but
if any have been inadvertently overlooked, the publishers will
be pleased to make the necessary arrangements at the first
opportunity.

Investigate business organisations

OBJECTIVES OF BUSINESS ORGANISATIONS

The focus in this unit is on business organisations and their objectives, legal obligations, types and structures. Modern businesses operate in a global market of seemingly endless opportunities and, at international level, the stakes are high. Companies want appropriate legal structures which offer recognition and protection on the one hand and freedom from unreasonable constraint or intervention on the other. Government policies provide support for business. Deregulation and the changes to company law are designed to encourage not only the establishment of British businesses but to attract major foreign investors too.

THE BUSINESS CONTEXT – UK PLC

Business is the lifeblood of a nation. Although the UK economy is very much market-led, it is still regarded as a mixed economy as there remains a significant, though much reduced, public or command sector. The economy has undergone extensive restructuring since the beginning of the 1980s. A major feature has been the vast programme of **privatisation**, transferring public utilities and nationalised industries from the public sector to the private sector. The dominant economic emphasis is on **wealth creation** and the **free market**; even in the National Health Service, education, and local government, the reorganisation and refocusing of budgets has encouraged competition. Britain is often referred to as UK plc.

This country is no longer reliant on manufacturing as its main source of wealth The **service sector** has grown so fast that it now contributes more than 60 per cent of gross domestic product (GDP). Despite the competition from the Singapore, Tokyo, New York and Frankfurt money markets, London is still predominant in banking, finance, and insurance. Tourism, too, has expanded giving the UK a multi-billion pound business. Growth has also been seen in the leisure, distribution, hotel and catering markets.

An economy is a dynamic framework and without a healthy enterprise sector there will not be sufficient tax revenues to invest in defence, roads, schools, social services and so on. Companies operate in a climate constantly challenged by change-agents and outside forces. They need to take account of **political**, **economic**, **social** and **technological (PEST)** policies, initiatives and developments. The role of government is open to conflicting political interpretations. Many would argue that its primary objective is to create the appropriate climate and regulatory framework in which business succeeds.

ACTIVITY

Since corporate taxes have been reduced, some companies have felt they should 'put something back' into the community. For some, it may be sponsoring the planting of flower beds in roundabouts; for others it might be the equipping of a specialist room in a school.

Discuss in a small group:

1 Whether or not you approve of this attitude.

2 How it benefits the community.

3 How it might benefit the donors.

4 Other examples of business sponsorship.

BUSINESS OBJECTIVES

Although people can work for themselves, offering a wide range of services and even products, isolated individuals are incapable of the mass production necessary to meet society's needs. Much business activity requires enormous investment and expertise. This can only be profitably managed by and through an organisation which assumes the responsibility for raising capital, co-ordinating resources, and driving projects forward to completion.

All organisations are set up with some clear purpose in mind. These objectives are essentially economic but they can also be social. The objectives of a company tend to be goal specific and can easily be measured; for example, an objective is to increase sales by five per cent. In contrast, aims are indications and intentions; for example, an aim is to become the market leader in Japan. The overriding objective for commercial companies must be **profit** or, in the case of not-for-profit organisations (such as co-operatives and charities), a surplus. However, the profit motive must be supported by other considerations like customer satisfaction. So, for example, shareholders expect British Gas to make a profit but the company is also required to ensure a safe and efficient gas supply to its consumers. Organisations in the public sector are required to break even but their objectives are, in the main, designed to meet the collective needs of society.

A company may state that its primary objective is to remain in business and to return a fair profit but the company may also want to emphasise other factors like **customer service**, **value for money**, **high quality products**; of course, attention to these factors obviously helps to create and build up business and profits. They also reflect a business attitude which the company can encourage through its administration and communications systems, and training programmes. A profitable business will not be achievable without a committed staff, reliability, quality assurance, and modern management and production techniques. Business leaders also argue that they require the minimum of government intervention.

The primary commercial objective then is profit, and its justification is that it rewards risk taking. Some businesses (such as oil, aerospace and pharmaceutical companies) invest very heavily in their projects and since there is a large market risk, sometimes even danger, a high profit is justified. The **net profit** – turnover less all costs and expenses – tends to be regarded as the reliable indicator of a company's performance. Net profit contributes to three charges:

- ☻ **company taxation;**

- ☻ **reserves;**

- ☻ **dividends to shareholders.**

The reserve fund is an important source of internal capital. It is the company's savings and strong reserves enable firms to invest in plans for growth, purchase equipment, build new facilities, and avoid applying to the bank for (expensive) development capital.

A key question about profit is whether it is to be maximised or optimised. **Maximising** means winning the largest possible profit from the market, but such a strategy can open a company to the risk of diminishing returns. While turnover and profit continue to increase, unit costs instead of falling may begin to rise. Returns, measured as profit as a percentage of turnover, begin to fall. **Optimising** means getting the best possible return, by generating profit as efficiently as possible. Companies might deny some addition to turnover growth if, by doing so, they can contain unit costs so that they continue to decline.

As we have emphasised, the profit motive, though crucial, is not the sole purpose of business. Some complementary business objectives may include:

- ☻ **to remain competitive and retain market share (which requires regular monitoring of costs, advertising, market research, product development, sales drives);**

- ☻ **to survive regardless of the prevailing economic climate even if it means the sale of assets;**

- ☻ **to respond to and respect environmental pressures (for example, by minimising pollution);**

- ☻ **to achieve customer satisfaction through reliable products or services and a high level of service;**

- ☻ **to offer value for money, through price consciousness and product development.**

Other factors may demand that a company redefines its goals, introduces new products and services, or even relocates to another country. A company needs to consider the external environment, paying attention to political, economic, social and technological developments (the PEST factors).

Public limited companies

Achieve the best possible financial return on capital

Build reserves

Satisfy shareholders and the market generally

Boost or maintain share market values

Optimise profits

Improve market share

Sole trader

Earn a living and be self-supporting

Charities

Increase income from collections, bequests and trading

Support chosen causes and projects

Win public (and government) sympathy for their work

National Health Service

Improve the general health of the nation

Treat more patients in less time

Use resources efficiently

FIGURE 2.1: Summary of primary objectives of different organisations.

ACTIVITY

List what you consider to be the aims and objectives of each of the following organisations:

⊗ **Prudential Assurance;**

⊗ **British Airways;**

⊗ **Marks & Spencer;**

⊗ **General Motors.**

LIMITED LIABILITY

Before looking at different types of companies, it is useful to begin with the important concept of **limited liability**. Limited liability is regarded as a privilege. It is a protection not against business loss but against unlimited personal loss. It is a major element in the legal structure of joint stock companies. Partnerships and sole traders cannot benefit from limited liability.

A working definition is that in the event of business failure, i.e. bankruptcy, a shareholder's financial liability is **limited** to the amount of capital invested or promised. If a shareholder invests £20,000 in either a public or a private limited company and then the company fails, all the shareholder can lose is that £20,000 investment. If, for example, a £50,000 investment has been made and only £15,000 has been contributed, the shareholder can be asked for the remaining £35,000. To illustrate the point, when British Telecom was privatised, investors paid for their shares in three tranches or instalments. The first payment secured ownership of the shares; therefore if British Telecom had soon gone under, shareholders would have been legally obliged to make the other two payments.

The essential point is that it is the company that goes bankrupt not the shareholders (although some may become bankrupt as a result). It is possible, therefore, for a joint stock company to be declared bankrupt for £200m but that does not mean the shareholders have to find that sum. The company's assets will be sold. If this sale of assets is not sufficient to meet the outstanding £200m liability, shareholders are not liable for the remaining debt. Their liability is limited to the size of their investment. In direct contrast, those business organisations which have no limited liability, such as partnerships and sole traders, must explore all ways of **meeting liabilities**. A sole trader's bankruptcy may mean the loss not just of the business but also his or her house, car and personal possessions to meet as much of the debt as possible.

Companies relying on the public subscription of shares know that limited liability is a strong selling point. It reduces the risk for individual investors and also attracts large-scale investment from financial institutions (pension funds, insurance companies, trade unions) which avoid taking excessive risks with their clients' or members' funds. Some companies may choose not to have limited liability. For example, a company limited by guarantee acquires the advantages of incorporation, but its members agree to meet certain sums in the event of failure.

TYPES OF OWNERSHIP

The economy is divided into **public** and **private** (or command and market) sectors. In the middle is the **mutuality sector** containing the not-for-profit organisations. Until recently, building societies would have appeared under this heading but, as a result of changes to the legal controls, societies are now free to compete with banks and other financial institutions on an equal footing. They are profit motivated and operate like public limited companies. Some are seeking registration as public limited companies; indeed, Abbey National is already quoted on the Stock Exchange and now ranks as one of Britain's largest banking operations.

The organisations in the mutuality sector certainly attempt to make a **trading surplus** and, in that sense, they are profit makers but with a difference – the profit supports the charitable or social aims of the organisation. In the case of mutual assurance societies (such as Norwich Union), the profits are ploughed back into the policies These societies are run without shareholders – the real owners are the **policy holders**.

PRIVATE SECTOR

THE JOINT STOCK COMPANY

A company is defined as an association of persons who contribute money (or equivalent value in goods and assets) to a common stock, employ it in some trade or business, and share the profit or loss arising that business. **Joint stock companies** are either public or private, and governed by and registered under the **Companies Act 1985**. A joint stock company has separate legal identity from its members and can sue or be sued in its own name. Both public and private companies require a minimum of only two members (there is no upper limit on members); each form enjoys limited liability.

THE PRIVATE COMPANY

This type of company is suitable for small and medium-sized operations. It is particularly suitable for family firms and for small enterprises involving just a handful of people. Some of its features are:

- ⊗ **it cannot advertise its shares for sale;**

- ⊗ **it is not quoted on the Stock Exchange;**

UK PLC		
Public sector (or command sector)	**Mutuality sector**	**Private sector** (or market sector)
Nationalised industries	Co-operatives	Public limited companies
Public corporations	Assurance societies	Private limited companies
Quangos	Friendly societies	Partnership
Local government	Charities	Sole traders
Central government		

FIGURE 2.2: Basic structure of the British economy.

- ☺ it is not obliged to publish its accounts;

- ☺ the company name ends with limited;

- ☺ it may have a sole director.

THE PUBLIC COMPANY

A public company is denoted by the letters 'plc' at the end of its name. All companies which are quoted on the Stock Exchange are **public limited companies**, but not all public limited companies are listed on the stock market (e.g. Co-operative Bank plc). To become a plc, a company must have an issued **share capital** of at least £50,000 and at least 25 per cent of the nominal value of the shares (and the whole of any premium) must have been received by the company. If the shares are nominally worth 10p (that is, the face value) but are sold at 50p, a company must have received 2.5p per share plus the premium of 40p. This regulation is to stop public limited companies setting up without sufficient capital. Other requirements include:

- ☺ it is a company limited by shares;

- ☺ its memorandum of association has a separate clause stating that it is a public company;

- ☺ it is obliged to publish an annual report and balance sheet;

- ☺ its shares are freely transferable, that is they can be bought and sold (through stockbrokers, banks and share shops).

The quoted companies can be tracked daily by reference to the Stock Exchange listings in financial pages of the broadsheet newspapers. The Stock Exchange is the **Official Listed Market (OLM)** for securities (shares). Companies which have traded for less than five years cannot join the OLM. However, if they have traded for more than three years, they may apply for admission to the **Unlisted Securities Market (USM)**.

ACTIVITY

Select five plcs which interest you and follow their share price movements over a four-week period. Imagine that you invested £1,000 in each company at the outset of the exercise. Determine your profits or losses.

REGISTRATION OF A COMPANY

The registration procedure is conducted by the **Registrar of Companies** who is an official of the Department of Trade and Industry (DTI). The Registrar must be satisfied that all statutory requirements have been fulfilled, and only then issues a **certificate of incorporation** which is conclusive evidence that a company complies with the law. It is an offence for a company to start trading or borrowing money until the certificate has been granted.

The law also requires that the company provides details of its internal rules and external relationships. It must submit two documents, the **memorandum of association** and the **articles of association**.

The memorandum of association defines the constitution and powers of the company and the scope of its activities. It includes:

- ☺ the name of the company including the word 'limited';

- ☺ the address of the registered office;

- ☺ a statement of the company's aims;

- ☺ the amount of capital the company wishes to raise;

- ☺ a statement that the shareholders' liability is limited.

The articles of association govern the internal rules of the company. The articles are a contract between the company and its shareholders in respect of their **ordinary rights** as members. The document must provide the details of:

- ☺ the nominal capital;

- ☺ when and how shareholders' meetings are to be conducted;

- ☺ the voting rights of members;

- ☺ how profits and losses will be distributed;

- ☺ the names of the directors;

- ☺ how the directors are appointed and the nature of their authority.

DIRECTORS

In law a company is regarded as 'an artificial legal person' which can only act by and through human agents. The **directors** are these agents; they are responsible to the shareholders for running the enterprise. They have the power to:

- **sell company assets;**

- **sue in the company's name;**

- **declare a dividend.**

They have two statutory duties:

- **to act as agents of the company – they are not personally liable if they act within their authority;**

- **to exercise the duty of trust.**

Directors are required to exercise their powers and responsibilities personally and collectively but the articles and memorandum authorise them to delegate to a managing director who is appointed to and answerable to the board. A director is a servant of the company and may delegate functions but not the exercise of discretion.

The actions of the directors are limited by the doctrine of *ultra vires* (meaning 'beyond the powers') which is a safeguard against the misuse of power and shareholders' money. The memorandum identifies the activities of the company and the directors cannot exploit any opportunities, however potentially profitable, which have been excluded. It is, however, normal practice for companies to write their objects wide enough to cover any reasonable business activity.

Directors may be executive – senior managers in the company with seats on the board – or non-executive, people outside the company but appointed to the board because they have particular expertise. If the company has borrowed from a merchant bank then the bank will often insist on one of its staff being appointed to the board to watch over the bank's interests. The shareholders may also be entitled to elect directors. A person who is an undischarged bankrupt may not be a director. There is an age limit of 70 for directors of public companies but a motion at the annual general meeting (AGM) can extend a director's service.

PARTNERSHIPS

Partnerships are governed by the **Companies Act 1985** and the **Partnership Act 1890**. Partners are bound by mutual trust and confidence. They are jointly and severally liable without limit (partners have no limited liability) for each other's actions. Thus, one partner's decision or action binds the other(s). The minimum membership is two and the maximum twenty but the Companies Act 1985 permits more for practices of accountants, solicitors and members of recognised stock exchanges. Every partner is entitled to participate in the management of the business.

According to the 1890 Act, a partnership dissolves on the death, resignation or bankruptcy of a partner, or on the agreed termination of the life and purpose of the business. In order to avoid disruption to the business, it is usual to draw up a **deed of partnership** which identifies the ways in which the partnership will be run. A deed might cover arrangements for sharing of profits, liabilities in case of debt, continuation after death or resignation of a member and so on. In the absence of a deed (or partnership articles), partnership activity will be governed by the 1890 Act.

The **Limited Partnership Act 1907** allows a partnership to claim limited liability for some of its partners, but there must be at least one general partner who is fully liable for all debts and obligations of the practice. This is not a common type of organisation – it is easier and more advantageous to set up a limited company.

You should note that is often the case that a person in a private business talks of another as 'my partner'. However, the term only has legal significance when referring to a partnership but it is widely used to describe associates in small businesses. Partnership is rarely used in any other context. One notable exception is the famous **John Lewis Partnership**, a leading retailer. John Lewis is a private company with a nominal share value of £100. It has four shareholders (the managing director has a 40 per cent holding and three trustees each hold 20 per cent). The company has a structure that encourages staff participation and the profits are shared in the form of bonuses by the staff. The term 'partnership' here reflects the democratic nature of John Lewis.

ACTIVITY

A partnership is not a particularly popular form of business organisation outside of the professions and specialised businesses. It is mainly suitable for bankers, architects, solicitors, accountants, financial advisers, stockbrokers and doctors. Bearing in mind the absence of limited liability, and the fact

that many of these businesses provide professional advice, suggest reasons why the partnership is appropriate for some professional people.

Sole traders

By **sole trader**, we mean self-employment. This is a very common form of business in the UK. In recent years, as more people have been made redundant or given early retirement, the number of sole traders has grown significantly. The sector continues to expand within the European Union at some at 2.5 per cent annually. Although most sole traders work on their own, it need not always be the case. Theoretically, a sole trader can employ hundreds of staff and own several factories but clearly the financial contribution and business risks would usually be too great. Typically sole traders are corner shopkeepers and market traders or have occupations such as self-employed plumbers, electricians, hairdressers and consultants.

The essential feature of this type of business is that the sole trader has full responsibility for the financial control of the business, for meeting capital requirements and the running costs, and full personal liability in the case of debt. There is a minimum of legal regulation. However, if the business is to be run under a name different to the proprietor's then registration is required under the **Business Names Act 1985**. The features of the sole trader are:

- ✪ **capital is only provided by the trader either from savings or a loan;**

- ✪ **direct personal involvement;**

- ✪ **unlimited liability;**

- ✪ **independence;**

- ✪ **easy to set up;**

- ✪ **entitlement to all of the profits but responsible for all of the debts;**

- ✪ **no requirement for the independent auditing of accounts.**

Franchises

A **franchise** is not a form of business organisation but a way of doing business. A sole trader or a limited company can undertake franchise operations. Franchising covers a variety of arrangements under which the owner of a product or service, or sometimes just a name, **licenses** other organisations or individuals to manufacture, use, or sell it in exchange for payment (in the form of fees, royalties or commissions). Usually the licensee benefits from an exclusive territory and support from the licenser in the form of staff training, advertising and promotion. The range of franchise activity is wide. It includes car dealerships, public houses, business services centres, doorstep milk deliveries, express delivery of parcels and fast food (Wimpy is a prime example).

ACTIVITY

Look for franchise offers in the business opportunities column of a Sunday newspaper.

1 **Make a list of what is available (type of business, capital required, potential earnings, etc.) and then devise an appropriate way of presenting the information.**

2 **If you were looking for a business opportunity suggest (with reasons) which franchise you would choose.**

FINANCING THE COMPANY

A private company cannot issue a prospectus because it cannot offer its shares to the public on the open market. It raises its **capital** by selling shares by private negotiation. A public company will issue its **prospectus** explaining to would-be shareholders the nature of the business, its markets and opportunities, and proposals for the future. That gives investors the chance to assess the company and the degree of risk.

The capital of a private or public company may be divided into **ordinary** or **preference shares**. Ordinary shares (or equities) carry the most risk. They rank after the preference shares when the profits are distributed. The ordinary shareholders are the true owners of a company and have most of the voting rights at company meetings. They receive a fluctuating **annual dividend** which depends upon the distributable profit after taxation and allocation to reserves. Depending on the financial performance of the company, dividends are not necessarily paid every year.

Shares have two values – the **nominal (face or par) value** and the **market value.** The nominal value is what the share is actually worth, the market value is the price investors are willing to pay for it. So a share in a major public limited company may be bought for, say, 350p but its nominal value might only be 25p. This means that in order to become a part-owner of the company, the investor must pay fourteen times the nominal value. The market price rises or falls according to market trends and business performance but the nominal value is fixed. Dividends are paid on nominal not market value.

Preference shares take priority over the ordinary shares and have the right to a **fixed dividend**. However, like ordinary shares, there is no automatic right to the payment, a company must have a profit to distribute. Preference shares may be cumulative or non-cumulative. If the shares are cumulative preference, and in any one year there is insufficient profit to pay the dividend, then the fixed dividend is carried forward and added to the dividend for the following year. A non-cumulative share has no right to payment in full nor for any arrears for years in which dividends were not paid.

Loan capital (debentures) interest has priority and must be paid whether the company has any distributable profits or not. If there are no profits the company is obliged to pay the **debenture holders** from the sale of assets, from capital, or by raising another loan.

ACTIVITY

1 Obtain the report and balance sheet of a well-known plc. Identify:
   (a) the nominal value of the ordinary shares;
   (b) the number of shares actually issued;
   (c) the numbers of shares it is entitled or authorised to issue.

2 Check the company in the Stock Exchange listings in the newspaper. Then:
   (a) note the current market value of the shares;
   (b) indicate whether the share price is rising or falling.

In addition to capital, businesses need other sources of finance. Even successful companies may require an arrangement with their bankers from time to time so that ongoing obligations such as wages, salaries and raw materials can be met. For most firms, the real financial anxiety is **cash flow**; they need working capital to sustain the life of the business. A company may have a full order book but it can run into difficulty if its customers do not pay on time (or at all). We will now consider some other sources of finance.

TRADE CREDIT
Credit is acquired by delaying the settlement of bills. The action gives a company 'breathing space' but it can result in suppliers refusing to do further business. In resolving a cash flow situation in this way, even temporarily, a company is effectively passing the problem back to its suppliers.

LEASING
Leasing is a popular means of providing cars for the sales force and executives. It is also used to acquire other equipment, including **office furniture** and **machinery**. The main advantages of leasing are:

- **a company does not have to commit a large proportion of its cash resources to obtain equipment;**
- **the cost of servicing the agreement comes out of revenue;**
- **payments are known in advance enabling better budgeting;**
- **the opportunity arises to update equipment regularly; for example, the car fleet need never be more than two years old, computers can be updated.**

BANK LOANS
Bank loans tend to be medium to long-term arrangements to finance major developments. Resorting to such loans may be avoided if the company has healthy reserve funds.

OVERDRAFT
An **overdraft** is usually a short-term arrangement used to meet current obligations. It is not suitable for an investment programme. Banks usually set a fairly low limit on the amount that can be borrowed on overdraft.

MUTUALITY SECTOR

THE CO-OPERATIVE SOCIETY

The most significant part of the mutuality sector is the **co-operative movement** which contains a diversity of businesses (agriculture, engineering, retail and wholesale distribution, travel, funeral services, property, banking) organised in **industrial** and **provident societies**. The co-operative movement celebrated its 150th anniversary in 1994. Its essential purpose was to create a social organisation to offer protection from unfair trading practices and poverty, The ultimate aim was to establish a 'commonwealth' owning the means of production, distribution and exchange.

In recent years, there has been a renewal of interest in the co-operative society as an ideal business form for self-governing workshops such as studios of artists, designers and printers. There is an umbrella organisation, **ICOM (Industrial Common Ownership Movement Ltd)**, which advises the co-operative development agencies and workers' co-operatives. It has a 'sister' organisation, **ICOF (Industrial Common Ownership Finance Ltd)**.

The essential features of a co-operative society are:

⊗ **it is registered under the Industrial and Provident Societies Acts 1965-78 and the Companies Acts;**

⊗ **it has limited liability;**

⊗ **shares are not transferable – they can only be bought from or sold to the society;**

⊗ **membership is available on the purchase of one share with a nominal value of £1;**

⊗ **the maximum shareholding depends upon the rules of each society but it cannot exceed the £15,000 limit set by the law;**

⊗ **membership is voluntary and open;**

⊗ **society control is democratic – each member is permitted one vote regardless of shareholding;**

⊗ **there is equitable use of any surplus or profit;**

⊗ **a limited rate of interest is paid on capital.**

Co-operative societies use various methods to distribute profits. After taxation and reserves, there is a distribution to members. Some money is put in a patronage fund to finance social and educational activities. Traditionally retail societies paid members a dividend on purchases, but currently there are four ways of rewarding members and societies may choose to apply one of the following:

⊗ **dividend on purchases;**

⊗ **trading stamps;**

⊗ **interest on the share account;**

⊗ **special offer vouchers for members.**

ACTIVITY

Obtain the latest published trading details of the co-operative movement (the retail societies, the Co-operative Wholesale Society, the Co-operative Bank and the Co-operative Insurance Society). The information should include turnover, trading surplus, members' benefits, the number of societies, shops, brand lines and members, assets, and premium income. Present your findings in a table.

CHARITIES

Because so many people give up their time to help, charities form part of what is known as the **voluntary sector**. They are run by full-time professionals and supported by a network of volunteers. There are more than 6,000 registered charities and voluntary organisations in the UK. They are financed by collections, flag days, donations, bequests and trading activities. Company sponsorship is also important, providing support such as rent-free accommodation, a minibus or the loan of a manager. The **National Lottery** also makes awards to selected charities.

Additionally, there are charitable trusts which can be found in both the private and public health and education sectors. These organisations operate as businesses but enjoy certain tax advantages.

ACTIVITY

Make a list containing ten charities known to you, putting them in what you regard as an order of priority.

FRIENDLY SOCIETIES

Friendly societies are not quite so well known today but, until the **Welfare State** was established, they were critical to some families who needed assistance during periods of illness or unemployment. The societies were formed for the mutual purpose of creating a fund to provide assistance to its members in time of need. In the 1930s, there were more than 3,000 societies, but today only a few hundred exist. Among the best known are the Royal Ancient Order of Buffaloes and the Ancient Order of Foresters.

ACTIVITY

Complete the tasks below for each of the following forms of business organisations: public company, private company, partnership, co-operative society and sole trader.

1 Identify the Act(s) of Parliament which control(s) its activities.

2 Describe the nature of its liability.

3 Suggest how its profits are distributed.

Present your answers in the form of a table.

PUBLIC SECTOR

The public sector contains the remaining nationalised industries and public corporations, central government ministries and departments, local authorities and quangos. Despite the transfer of many activities from the public to the private sector, it remains a large sector of activity.

PRIVATISATION PROGRAMME

The justification for the massive programme of privatisation (which began in the early 1980s) is that companies in the private sector are more efficient than those in the public sector. It is argued that they produce a better level of service because of the pressure of **market forces** and the need to meet **profit-related targets**. The government has tried to inject **market disciplines** to the rest of the public sector by the creation of internal markets and profit centres within the remaining public bodies and organisations. Since 1979, more than thirty public enterprises have been transferred to the private sector. *Fig 2.3* demonstrates the impact of the privatisation policy. It lists the major assets which each realised more than £1bn when privatised.

Asset	£bn
British Airports Authority	1.2
British Gas	6.5
British Petroleum	6.1
British Steel	2.4
British Telecom	4.8
Britoil	1.1
Cable and Wireless	1.0
Electricity distribution companies	5.2
Rolls-Royce	1.0
Water companies	5.2
Total revenue	**34.5**

FIGURE 2.3: Assets realised by major privatisation sales since 1979.

Under current government proposals, there are still some major public sector enterprises which will either be sold off eventually or turned into profitable businesses within the public sector. British Rail is in the process of being privatised. It has been split up into a number of companies in preparation for the transfer to the private sector. There are separate companies for ownership of the track, operation of the rolling stock, and so on. Other public enterprises include London Transport, Nuclear Electric and the Post Office. It is considered that market forces will encourage cost effective organisations and lead to the better use of resources.

ACTIVITY

Discuss in a group the view that the gas, water and electricity companies, which control essential resources, should have remained in the public sector under the supervision of the government rather than have been transferred to the private sector and, thereby, been subject to market forces.

CENTRAL GOVERNMENT

Central government comprises ministries and departments which set policy for and, in many cases, administer public services. Government activity has to be funded from **taxation** and other sources. It raises revenue from personal and corporate taxation, indirect taxes (VAT, customs and excise duties), sale of public assets (privatisation), motor vehicle tax, national insurance contributions and national savings. The government also borrows money. **Gilt-edged stock** is issued, enabling investors to loan money to the government. Some financial contributions may be made by the **European Union**, particularly to assist declining areas (where, for example, traditional coal, steel and shipbuilding industries have run down) with employment creation projects.

LOCAL GOVERNMENT

Local government is an important element in the country's democratic structure. Councils and local authorities are responsible for education, social services, police, fire, consumer protection, public transport, highways, allotments, leisure and recreation. Local government is funded by the **council tax**, **government grants**, **loans** and **charges for its services**. Business rates are levied on all commercial properties and paid to central government. This money is reallocated to local councils in accordance with a formula based on population and the level of services. District councils are the **tax raising authorities**.

Privatisation affects local government too. Its role is changing from one of providing services to one of enabling those services to be delivered. One characteristic of this change is **compulsory competitive tendering** (CCT). This policy requires certain services to be put out to tender, that is other organisations have the right to submit a bid to carry out those services (examples include refuse collection, grass cutting and management of leisure services). Council departments are entitled to bid for the contracts, but only in their own areas; they are unable, under the law, to bid for contracts elsewhere – unlike private sector contractors.

ACTIVITY

When the council sends your household its demand for the council tax, it is accompanied by a leaflet explaining the provision and costs of local authority services. Obtain the latest version of this leaflet from your local council. Then:

1 **List the services in declining order of expenditure (for the current year).**

2 **Note (or calculate) the average charge per council taxpayer.**

3 **Identify the total cost of running your local authority.**

4 **Explain what is meant by the 'capping limit'.**

5 **Suggest who might be eligible for council tax discounts or exemptions.**

QUANGOS

Quango stands for quasi-autonomous non-governmental organisation. Their justification is that ministers (and their departments) need some assistance in the formulation and application of their policies, so lay people with particular expertise are appointed to give advice. There are some 40,000 public appointments to quangos; approximately 10,000 people are appointed or re-appointed every year. The work can be unpaid or paid, and varies from one day a month to a full-time commitment. Examples of quangos include tribunals, public corporations (such as the BBC) and advisory bodies (on, for example, the environment, health and agriculture). Anyone can submit an application to the **Public Appointments Unit**. The unit circulates a list to the various government departments which are responsible for the appointments.

ORGANISATIONAL STRUCTURES

Management works through a framework of responsibility and authority which **co-ordinates resources**, **monitors performance**, **resolves problems** and **achieves targets**. Management is a function which exists regardless of the size of a business organisation, although a management structure usually becomes more obvious the larger the company. The sole trader (see *Fig. 2.4*) operates as sales manager, finance director, customer services manager (and more) – in reality, one person is trying to get work, to satisfy the customers and to manage the business – but these functions become highly specialised in larger organisations. The sole trader may take on an assistant to help out but the agreement about terms will most likely be verbal and even casual. Compare that to seeking a job with ICI or Ford, where the recruitment process is well defined and organised by professional and qualified people. Although the business functions remain the same regardless of structure, size and the nature of the business, the degree of specialisation varies between different organisations.

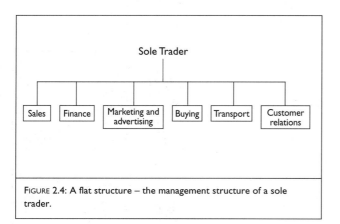

FIGURE 2.4: A flat structure – the management structure of a sole trader.

Businesses can be classified by the number of people involved:

- ⊗ **micro** – **less than 10 staff**
- ⊗ **small** – **11 to 99 staff**
- ⊗ **medium** – **100 to 499 staff**
- ⊗ **large** – **500 plus staff**

The size of a company largely determines the shape of the organisation. In a smaller firm, the staff have to be more flexible and multi-skilled. Participation in a micro business is a very hands-on affair. Like the sole trader model in *Fig. 2.4*, the structure is probably a straight line as the boss is closely involved in the day-to-day activities. In a small crop-spraying and air taxi business, for example, the owner is probably the sales director and the chief (and only) pilot, while the receptionist is also the bookkeeper and the secretary. Technical support is offered by a mechanic who services the plane, mows the airstrip, paints the hangar and runs errands. The ways in which an organisation's objectives are to be met must be considered in the context of the most appropriate structure.

FORMS OF ORGANISATIONAL STRUCTURE

Organisational structures can be classified under a number of headings. Before discussing the basic forms, it is worth emphasising that, in practice, hybrid forms exist – in other words, a structure may be basically one form but will assume aspects of another. It should also be acknowledged that, although a structure may be sound, people will always find ways to challenge it and promote their own agenda. Equally, in a complex system, they will find informal ways to make it work.

Received wisdom suggests that the logical division of a company's structure is by function but, in many cases, division by product might more appropriate. A multinational conglomerate might divide up according to country, broad geographical area, or by company. None of these approaches is absolutely standard – a division by product may, for example, require sub-division by function, with some other functions remaining centralised. The titles or ranks people have, the tasks they perform, their areas of responsibility and the extent of their authority, all depend upon the size, culture and organisational structure of the company for which they work.

LINE

Line structures are the simplest of all the structures and perhaps the most familiar. With a line structure, a company is usually organised by **functional departments** (personnel, marketing, production, sales, etc.) with each headed by a senior manager. The main characteristic is that there is a **line of responsibility** and authority (see *Fig. 2.5*) which decreases in power as it goes down through the structure from the managing director or chief executive officer to the unskilled manual employee. Each level of management, supervision or operation is answerable to the one above. It is an **hierarchical structure**, simple to understand, and staff know precisely where they are in it and to whom they are responsible. It also offers an uncomplicated way of delegating tasks, monitoring performance and imposing discipline. The downside is that it may encourage strict demarcation between departments and an authoritarian management style.

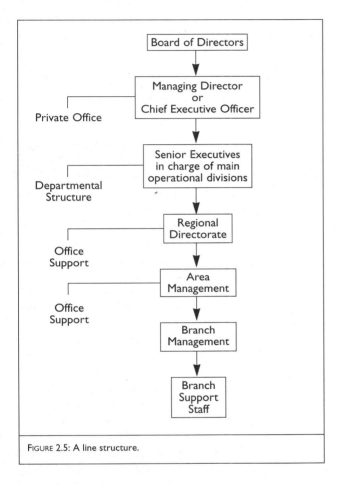

FIGURE 2.5: A line structure.

FUNCTIONAL

In a functional structure, the flow of responsibility and authority is determined by function with little reference to departmental structure. Each function of the business is managed by a specialist whose authority can carry more weight than that of the line manager in whose area that function is being partially or totally carried out. This structure has the effect of reducing the authority of line management. These issues can be resolved if the functional manager liaises with the line manager so there is no confusion in line command, discipline and organisation.

Functional managers are freed from day-to-day routine management concerns and can concentrate on their areas of expertise. Because they have access to all areas of a company, they are able to contribute advice and observation on the co-ordination of the organisation's activities. This structure is flexible and specialists can respond quickly to external or internal change-agents.

LINE AND STAFF

Essentially, this is a combination of the line and functional forms but the specialists, the functional managers, have advisory rather than executive authority. In a sense, they are **trouble-shooters** who can attend to problems arising in those departments requiring their services. However, since they are appointed because of their experience and knowledge, their advice, though not binding, is usually regarded as persuasive.

A line and staff structure may encourage clashes of personality and opinion, affecting efficiency and morale. However, a specialist who is known for sound and practical advice, depth of knowledge and good personal administration will be well regarded by staff at all levels; there should be no confusion about areas of authority.

COMMITTEE

A committee structure is a familiar form in local government (see *Fig. 2.6*) where each area of the council's activity (education, public works, finance, etc.) is governed by a committee comprising elected councillors and senior council officers. The committees do not **manage**, they **determine policy**. It is left to the officers to exercise their management roles in their departments.

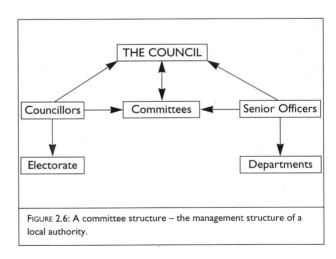

FIGURE 2.6: A committee structure – the management structure of a local authority.

The committee style has been used increasingly in business in recent years as it encourages **employee participation**. It affords the opportunity for issues to be openly debated resulting in better balanced, informed and representative decisions. Committees may be either executive or advisory. The purpose of any committee must be clearly defined before it is set up.

In many ways, the committee system is less a form of organisation but rather an approach within another structure. The use of committees and the value placed on their recommendations will reflect the culture of the company.

MATRIX

In a matrix structure, each function within an organisation is placed under the direction of a functional manager who leads a team of specialists. These specialists are also located in departments under the supervision of line managers. Each specialist is, therefore, subject to two sources of authority – the functional manager who is charged with technical performance and targets, and the line manager whose concern is with staff management.

In a matrix, people are grouped in divisions or teams according to their areas of expertise. It is possible for a person to be responsible to several team leaders, some of whom may even be of lower status. So, in addition to being accountable to the functional and line managements, a specialist may be a member of one or more **inter-disciplinary project teams**.

The matrix ought to encourage the ready **cross-fertilisation** of experience, knowledge and opinion leading to the better use of intellectual resources.

ACTIVITY

Draw up the structure of an organisation familiar to you (your college or company). Comment on its features (for example, it might be basically committee with elements of functional). Indicate whether, in your opinion, it is a suitable form in which the organisation can deliver its aims and objectives and also motivate its staff.

CENTRALISATION

Centralisation is the practice of concentrating all the power – the responsibility and authority – at the top of an organisation. Typically, this places power with the managing director but also with a **senior management team (SMT)**. Centralisation arises in complex organisations with widespread activities as there is a need to keep control of the organisation and to ensure that policies are properly carried out.

The disadvantages of centralisation can be seen as:

- ⊗ **removing initiative from supervisory and middle management;**

- ⊗ **demanding that all actions and decisions be approved by the SMT;**

- ⊗ **creating a bureaucracy with formal procedures;**

- ⊗ **encouraging reactive rather pro-active staff;**

- ⊗ **encouraging a lack of commitment to the overall aims of the company.**

Centralisation is administratively convenient and allows absolute control over the organisation. Although a company may have many divisions, departments or activities, certain functions will remain under firm central control to ensure uniformity, tight budget control, elimination of waste and avoidance of duplicate stock. Centralised functions may include computing, personnel, accounts, reprographics and purchasing.

DECENTRALISATION

In a decentralised structure, the responsibility for various functions and operations is devolved from the top and rests wherever the action is. It places decision-making and initiative directly in the hands of managers and supervisors. Decentralisation challenges standardised procedures, even the uniform application of policy. But it can encourage the setting up of action teams with **local autonomy** and their own targets. It can offer **flexibility of operation** and delivery.

ACTIVITY

Working in a group, define the following terms (which have been used in the text) within a business context:

- ⊗ **authority;**

- ⊗ **responsibility;**

- ⊗ **efficiency;**

- ⊗ **effectiveness;**

- ⊗ **management.**

PORTFOLIO ASSIGNMENT

This assignment is an investigation into business organisation. You are to compile a report which will examine and compare the structures, motives, and differences of three selected business organisations.

Choose three business organisations to investigate – one must come from the public sector and two from either the private sector or one from each of the mutuality and private sectors.

Select organisations which readily offer the required information and which are interesting. Plcs are required to make their report and balance sheets available to any enquirer (who may be a prospective shareholder) but it may be difficult to access information about a private company (unless you go to Companies House and ask to see the articles and memorandum).

Your report needs to be divided into three areas of investigation.

1 For each selected organisation, offer a general explanation of its broad financial objectives. Emphasis should be given to the earning and distributing of profit and/or surplus.

2 The overall objectives of each organisation must be defined. This should be supported by an explanation of how the financial, legal and controlling (management and structural) differences between organisations influence the achievement and outcome of those objectives.

3 Construct organisational charts illustrating the different structures of the companies. Support the charts with clear explanations of the differences and highlight recent, planned or likely changes to either structures, locations or functions.

Investigate administration systems

The word **'administration'** has several meanings. In the context of this unit, it means all the various **formal information systems** that a business uses to support the organisation and its functions and ensure that it achieves its objectives. For example, the finance department of a supplier formally informs a customer how much money she or he has to pay for goods by sending an invoice; by getting money in from the customer on time, it makes an important contribution to the business achieving its objectives.

A business organisation survives by generating more income from sales than it costs to provide a product or service. It has to operate efficiently to achieve that objective. A key task of management is to design an **effective organisational structure** which brings together all the necessary functions and resources, and sets realistic objectives so that all employees are clear about their contribution to the success of the organisation.

Equally important to the efficiency of a business is the design of systems that provide specific and accurate information to all parts of the organisation and to customers and to suppliers. These are described as **'administration systems'** or sometimes **'paperwork systems'**.

ADMINISTRATION SYSTEMS

Administration is the process of:

- ⊗ **gathering information (input);**
- ⊗ **processing information;**
- ⊗ **storing information;**
- ⊗ **and distributing information (output).**

Note that the terms **input** and **output** are more readily associated with computer-based systems, but they are equally applicable here. They are considered in more detail later in this unit.

FIGURE 2.7: The administrative process.

Information is the raw material of decision making. Managers make critical decisions based on the information provided by administration systems. It is, therefore, important that information is:

- ⊗ **accurate;**
- ⊗ **on time;**
- ⊗ **sufficient;**
- ⊗ **cost effective.**

Systems that produce information that is specifically designed to aid managers in decision making are often called **management information systems (MIS)**.

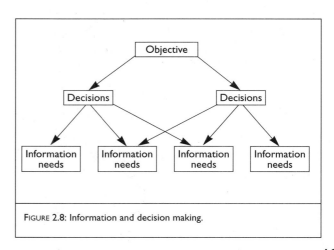

FIGURE 2.8: Information and decision making.

Managers of small businesses depend less on formal systems than managers of large companies. This is because there are relatively few transactions in a small business, the manager is familiar with all aspects of the business and, therefore, 'knows what is going on'.

In contrast, large businesses might generate millions of transactions, have a wide range of products or services and operate on many sites. Their senior managers need well-designed administration and information processing systems that supply them with accurate, timely information upon which they can make high-level decisions.

As businesses grow, the demand for better and faster information grows too. Ensuring that administration systems can grow with the organisation is important if the company is to continue to satisfy its customers.

It is worth noting that all administration creates an **overhead cost** – it does not add value to the product or service that the organisation provides to its customers. Administration systems should be adequate but not excessive – that is, they should be cost effective and provide value for money.

However, companies are required to maintain some administration systems by law; for example Pay As You Earn (PAYE) records must be maintained and returns made on Inland Revenue forms. VAT records are mandatory. Accidents must be recorded and serious incidents must be reported to the Health and Safety Executive. But these systems, too, should be **economic** and **efficient**.

PROCESSING INFORMATION

All business organisations, large and small, must process data. They will do so manually, with computers, or using calculators. There is a wide variety of tailor-made business machines for particular applications such as accounting, manufacturing and so on. The output information can be distributed on paper, electronically to visual display units (VDUs), by fax, by phone and by computer disc.

ACTIVITY

Design a simple questionnaire to get evidence from your head of department (or equivalent) of the ways data is processed within your department at school or college. Give it a reference number (for example, item 1) and write an index to keep track of

your evidence. If you can gather any forms or flow diagrams of the actual systems, give them reference numbers and file them in the same way.

Put the completed questionnaire (and other documents) in a folder of evidence which may be useful in the assignment at the end of this element.

INDEX		
Item No	Description of item	Type of evidence
1	Methods of data processing use in department	Questionnaire completed by head of department

The speed and extent of **electronic communication** is a great asset to multinational businesses and is beginning to permit trans-European administration. So, several companies in Europe that belong to the same group or parent company might set out to share the same services and systems. At present, the business areas that lend themselves to this approach, mainly because of European laws and regulations, are:

- ✪ **human resources;**

- ✪ **environment;**

- ✪ **health and safety;**

- ✪ **information technology;**

- ✪ **business services;**

- ✪ **public and government affairs;**

- ✪ **tax;**

- ✪ **purchasing.**

You can see where this is leading. If these administration systems are common across country boundaries, the parent company only needs one administration centre (or head office) in Europe to run all their businesses. Companies within the group will only need terminals linked to the centre, and they will not need any administration staff or senior management, just operational managers. Think of the costs that could be saved in this way.

☀️ ACTIVITY

The organisation in which you study – your school or college – will have administration systems to support its work. It will have systems to register students and ensure they are on the correct course; it will have systems to record all financial transactions and record income and expenditure; it will have systems to keep personnel records for all lecturers and other staff; and it may have systems to keep track of customers (students) and keep them informed about the college's services.

Bearing in mind that college administration staff are busy and have a demanding job to do, try to arrange for someone from the administration department to outline the systems that are used in the organisation. At this stage, try to get a big picture of all the systems and how they carry accurate, specific information from one department to another for the purpose of managing the affairs of the school or college effectively.

Fig. 2.9 looks at some administration activities that might result from a student applying to study Advanced Business GNVQ at a college.

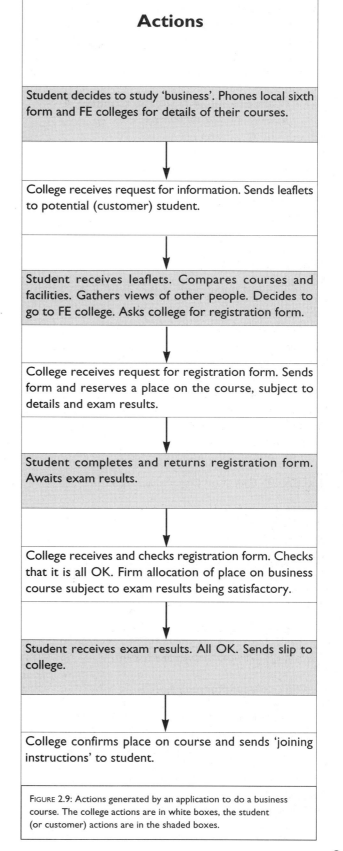

Actions

Student decides to study 'business'. Phones local sixth form and FE colleges for details of their courses.

↓

College receives request for information. Sends leaflets to potential (customer) student.

↓

Student receives leaflets. Compares courses and facilities. Gathers views of other people. Decides to go to FE college. Asks college for registration form.

↓

College receives request for registration form. Sends form and reserves a place on the course, subject to details and exam results.

↓

Student completes and returns registration form. Awaits exam results.

↓

College receives and checks registration form. Checks that it is all OK. Firm allocation of place on business course subject to exam results being satisfactory.

↓

Student receives exam results. All OK. Sends slip to college.

↓

College confirms place on course and sends 'joining instructions' to student.

FIGURE 2.9: Actions generated by an application to do a business course. The college actions are in white boxes, the student (or customer) actions are in the shaded boxes.

In this example, action will not be confined to the college administration department. In processing the application, the administration department will:

- advise the head of business that a place is allocated;

- request funding from the County Education Department;

- provide the senior management team with details of enrolments;

- set up central records for each student with all personal and course details.

As a result of this information, other people in the organisation and in associated organisations take some action.

The head of the business department must:

- allocate staff to teach the course;

- allocate a classroom for the course;

- allocate materials and books;

- prepare the course register;

- prepare the student record.

The County Education Department will:

- gather data about all students going to the college;

- make an appropriate award of funds to the college;

- advise central government about student numbers and use of funds.

The college's senior management team:

- receives information about total numbers of students in each department;

- reviews resources and budgets with each head of department;

- reallocates resources according to student numbers.

In addition, as students accept places, the college's administration department needs to:

- put all students' details on records;

- put all courses' details on records;

- make allocation of lockers, etc.;

- issue travel vouchers as appropriate.

ACTIVITY

What might have been the scene on the first day of the new term had the administration system failed to correctly record the number of students joining the business course?

Equally, what would it be like if the head of department had received the information too late to complete the necessary planning?

Consider the following questions.

1 How would the students (customers) have felt?

2 What opinion would the students (customers) have of the organisation?

3 How would the inaccuracies affect the head of department?

4 How would the inaccuracies affect the County Education Department?

5 How would the inaccuracies affect the decisions made by the senior management team?

6 Draw conclusions about the relationships between administration systems and the efficiency of an organisation.

ACTIVITY

Gather all the forms that are used in your school's or college's enrolment system. Paste them on a large sheet of paper in the order in which they are completed. (You might find it helpful to use flip chart – A1 size – paper.) Draw lines that show the flow of data and information, just like a flow chart.

1 Can you identify the input data and the output information?

2 How is the data processed?

3 Write a short step-by-step description of the system so that a new member of staff would be able to follow it without too much help. Test it out on a friend or relative. Did she or he understand it?

4 Now give your chart and description a reference and file them with the rest of your evidence.

FUNCTIONAL ADMINISTRATION SYSTEMS

Most businesses involve four key functions: **production**, **finance**, **marketing** and **personnel**. *Fig. 2.10* shows the administration systems that might be found in each of these four main functions.

Fig. 2.10 shows the great variety of administration systems needed to support a business organisation. Each of these systems could be run in a 'stand alone' fashion with its own paperwork and procedures. However, there is often data which is common to several systems and, where that occurs, it should be possible to find links between two or more systems. Modern information technology allows systems that have common information needs to share the same database. By linking them, businesses can reduce some duplication of effort. For example:

⊗ the production section needs some raw materials, so a material requisition is raised and given to the storekeeper;

⊗ stores issues the items and updates the stock records;

⊗ if the stock records show that the item is running low, stores will raise a purchase requisition to tell the purchasing section that the item needs replacing;

⊗ purchasing will raise a purchase order to replenish the item concerned.

FUNCTION	ADMINISTRATION SYSTEMS
Production	Production control system; drawings control system; purchase order system; stock control system; quality control system; planned maintenance system; machine utilisation system.
Finance	Credit control; sales invoicing; sales ledger; purchase ledger; petty cash; wages and salaries; PAYE records; statutory payment records; budgetary control; final accounts.
Marketing	Sales budgeting; sales recording; customer analysis; product analysis; territory analysis; promotion scheduling and purchasing; marketing budget control; customer communication systems; sales and marketing analysis and reporting system.
Personnel	Recruitment and selection systems; employee records; performance review systems; accident records; attendance records; training records; training budgeting; salary and wages control systems; staff turnover system.

FIGURE 2.10: Functional administration systems.

In this example the same information – the name and reference number of the item on the documents mentioned – has been reproduced four times for different purposes. By designing all four systems together as an integrated system, it is possible to reduce or eliminate duplication.

ACTIVITY

Examine the lists of functional administrative systems in *Fig 2.10* and note down which systems might be found in each of the following organisations:

- a sole trader selling and fitting kitchen furniture;

- a small limited company employing thirty-seven people providing packaged holidays in Europe;

- a plc manufacturing washing machines, refrigerators and spin dryers;

- a co-operative retail company selling a wide range of food and household goods;

- the planning and maintenance department of a local council;

- Save the Children Fund.

Consider the relationship between type and size of organisation, and the need for administrative systems.

PROCESS AND PROCEDURES

The term 'administrative process' relates to the way things are done. It might be:

- a manual process or an automated process;

- a paper-based process or an electronic process;

- an independent process or an integrated process.

Most administration systems are now **automated** and **electronic**, even in the smallest organisations, although many still produce paper outputs and are not yet fully integrated.

Administration systems are formal communications carrying specific information around the organisation. There is a need for accuracy and timeliness. It follows that people cannot just do what they like. There must be a strict procedure which ensures all the actions that need to be taken are taken in the right order. Every administration system has a procedure which contributes to its effectiveness.

Administration systems gather, process (sometimes store) and distribute information. These are distinct stages in the process but, in addition, many systems cross boundaries between departments, sections, and often between organisations. *Fig. 2.11* shows how a sales order invoicing system might operate.

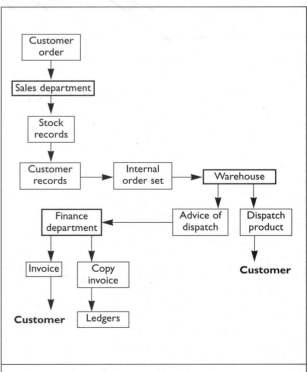

FIGURE 2.11: Sales order invoicing system.

You should notice that processing a customer's order has several stages:

1 **Check stock levels. If available, the process can continue; if not, some further supplies would have to be manufactured.**

2 **Check customer record. If the customer's credit OK, continue; if not, pass back to sales department to deal with.**

3 **Raise paperwork. Tell the warehouse to pack and dispatch the goods.**

4 **The warehouse dispatches the goods and advises finance that they have been sent out.**

5 **Finance raises an invoice for the goods.**

6 **The invoice is posted to the customer. A copy is sent to the ledgers.**

ACTIVITY

Think about the differences between a process and a procedure.

1 **Give three examples of processes that you find in your studies. An example is the assessment process.**

2 **Give three examples of procedures that you may come across in your school or college. One example is the enrolment procedure.**

3 **How are processes and procedures different?**

4 **Give three reasons for having processes and three reasons for having procedures.**

SUITABILITY

In this section, we look at the suitability of administrative systems. In looking at suitability, we consider **fitness for purpose**, **value for money**, **security** and **health and safety**.

FITNESS FOR PURPOSE

Some systems are best carried out using a pen and a printed form. For example, many doctors write out a prescription for the patient to take it to a chemist to be made up. However, in some larger practices doctors have computer terminals on their desks which hold each patient's records. Simply by typing in the patient's surname and initials, the doctor can access a record of all the drugs at present being prescribed for a patient, and simply produce a new or repeat prescription. The system then 'looks up' the costs of the drugs prescribed on a database, and updates the doctors drugs budget.

Other systems are very sophisticated and rely on massive remote databases. For example, when you book an airline ticket, the travel clerk takes your requirements and accesses a database from a desktop terminal. The database holds details of every flight – the seating capacity of each flight, the number of seats that have already been booked and who has made the booking. The clerk finds a flight that meets your needs, and if it meets your requirements, books a seat on the flight and issues your ticket . The ticket is a small form containing about four copies of the booking. The database is immediately updated to prevent that seat being sold twice. Another clerk hundreds of miles away can access the database at the same time but cannot double book your seat. (Some of you may have had a different experience and found that your seat on an aircraft had been double booked. This is probably not a computer error but a policy that some companies have to overbook by a certain percentage to take account of the people who do not turn up. This policy is designed to prevent aircraft flying with unnecessarily empty seats, which costs airlines revenue.)

In setting up a new administration system, there are many questions a designer needs to ask:

⊗ **what does the user want/need?**

⊗ **what is the purpose/objective of the system?**

⊗ **what is the input to the system?**

- who will input data and how?

- is it a one-input system or a multi-input system?

- how will the data be processed?

- how will the data be stored?

- what outputs from the system are required?

- how will the output be presented?

Factors that influence the system design and the way that data is processed are:

- the size of organisation;

- the nature of its business;

- the time available for the transaction to be completed;

- the nature of the transaction being administered.

A trader dealing in commodities might simply write a note in a notebook; the deal is instant and traders rely on the creed that 'my word is my bond'. In a fish market, simply sticking a printed number on a crate of fish might be enough to ensure it reaches the correct destination. There is no time or facility for anything else.

Buying something from a shop using a credit card simply requires your signature on a slip of paper for security reasons. All the other procedures are usually done electronically at high speed:

- your credit balance is checked;

- the card is checked to ensure it has not been lost, stolen or is out of date;

- the transaction is recorded;

- your account is debited.

It is relatively straightforward to test whether an administrative system is 'fit for the purpose'. The test is 'does it do what it was intended to do' or 'does it achieve its objectives'.

For example, in credit card transactions a system would be deemed 'fit for its purpose' if it enabled customers to pay for purchased goods quickly, accurately and securely.

ACTIVITY

You are probably involved with administration systems every day. For example, if you travel to college by bus or train there is an administration system for collecting fares and giving you a ticket. Similarly, if you buy something in a shop, you will pay for it and receive a receipt. Taking a book from the library is another example.

1 List six different examples of activities you have been involved with in the last week that had its own administration system.

2 For each one, draw a simple diagram showing what happened. For example:
   (a) Got on bus near home
   (b) Paid driver 50p
   (c) Driver gave me a ticket for 35p
   (d) Stayed on the bus as far as college
   (e) Got off bus.

3 Comment on the 'fitness for purpose' of each system.

VALUE FOR MONEY

It is much more difficult to determine whether a system is 'value for money'. In the past, when paperwork systems were manually processed, it was possible to draw a flow diagram and work out the cost of each stage in terms of clerical labour, the materials used, postage, etc. It was possible to say with some confidence how much it cost, for example, to raise and process a purchase order for an item of raw material stock, and to store the item until it was needed.

It is, however, much more difficult with computerised systems. There are some complex issues that would most probably require the expert input of an accountant:

- ⊗ is the computer hired, leased or bought?

- ⊗ how is the cost to be depreciated?

- ⊗ what is the cost of the software?

- ⊗ what is the cost of hardware maintenance?

- ⊗ what is the cost of the software maintenance?

- ⊗ what is the cost of training both the administrators and the managers?

- ⊗ what is the cost of installation?

- ⊗ what is the cost of security?

- ⊗ what is the cost of consumables?

- ⊗ how are the total costs to be apportioned to each system?

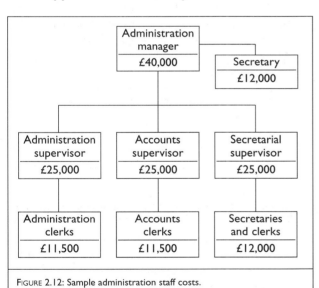

FIGURE 2.12: Sample administration staff costs.

 **ACTIVITY**

Form a discussion group of three or four colleagues.

1 Using the evidence already filed in your folder from previous activities, discuss all the information you would need to do a thorough costing of a system. Start with how you might obtain information about the costs of the equipment being used to process the data.

2 Decide how you might calculate the costs of installation.

3 Think how you might calculate the ongoing running costs. *Fig. 2.12* shows some typical salary costs for administration work.

4 When your group has discussed the topic, write a memo for a manager highlighting the costs of the administration system.

SECURITY

There are three aspects to security in administration systems:

- ⊗ security of information;

- ⊗ security of electronic data files;

- ⊗ security of finance.

SECURITY OF INFORMATION

In most organisations there is some information that is open; anyone can know it. For example, **open information** would include the prices of a company's products; the contents of food products, etc. Some information has to be disclosed by law. But there is some **sensitive information** that a company would not like its competitors to know. For example, firms would not wish to disclose the costs of producing its products or the secret recipe that makes its food taste better or different from others in the same market.

And there is information that is classified, which only certain people may know about. For example, **classified information** would include a patient's records in a doctor's surgery or hospital, a plan to take-over another company, or to develop a revolutionary new product.

Where this information could be gleaned from an administration system, there will be restrictions placed on the distribution of that information – only certain, specified people may have access to it. Documents will be marked clearly if they are confidential, restricted or secret. The government enforces secrecy of some of its data by the **Official Secrets Act**.

SECURITY OF ELECTRONIC DATA FILES

There are two types of security needed for files. First, security against loss of data caused by physical, electrical or electronic failure. This security is usually achieved by keeping copies of all critical files in a fireproof safe, and by holding 'father' and 'grandfather' files which could be updated to get back lost data.

Second, an organisation needs security against corruption of files by virus programs. This can be achieved by passing all new files through a virus check before they are loaded.

These issues are explained more fully in element 2.4 later in this unit.

ACTIVITY

Prepare a short talk of about five minutes (to be presented to your class colleagues) that sets out the moral arguments about either:

(a) the rights of people to security for their personal data held in computers; or

(b) the practice of 'hacking' into other people's computer files.

SECURITY OF FINANCE

It is said that money makes rogues of us all. That may not be true, but certainly companies have to guard against **theft** and **financial malpractice**. All administration systems that relate to receiving or spending the company's money must be designed to avoid theft or fraud. The accounting professional bodies lay down strict guidelines to be followed in this regard. All systems must be auditable; that is, all money due to a company, and all money spent by a company must be traceable by means of an audit trail.

ACTIVITY

Prepare a short questionnaire that can be given to your school or college accountant. Ask two or three questions that enquire about the ways – internal and external – that money is kept secure.
Give the completed questionnaire a reference number and file it in your folder.

HEALTH AND SAFETY AT WORK

There are certain things in the administration environment (as opposed to the production environment) that should be considered when planning, designing and implementing administration systems. Although the **Health and Safety at Work Act 1974** is the main statute employers must comply with, **The Offices, Shops and Railway Premises Act 1963** also relates to safety in offices. The main provisions of these Acts relating to offices are:

- each person sitting at a desk should have 40 sq. ft of floor space or 400 cubic feet of space;

- the temperature should be at least 16°C or 60°F within the first hour of work;

- there should be sufficient toilets and washing facilities;

- lighting should be adequate;

- seating should be appropriate to the job;

- ventilation should be adequate particularly where machinery (for example, some photocopiers) gives off fumes;

- fire exits should be clearly marked and access to them free from obstruction.

The **Health and Safety Executive (HSE)** provides advice about the use of visual display units (VDUs). The key points are:

- ☺ jobs should be designed to allow short, frequent breaks;

- ☺ screens should be adjustable to suit individuals needs;

- ☺ bright lights should not reflect in the screen;

- ☺ screens should not have a window or bright light behind them;

- ☺ the characters should not flicker.

Failure to comply with the Health and Safety at Work Act is a criminal offence. The HSE consider that managers who control the resources are responsible for safety. Employees are required to co-operate with employers on health and safety matters.

ACTIVITY

Walk around your school or college and note all the things that are in place to keep people safe and healthy. For example, there will be fire extinguishers and fire exits.

If you can arrange it, ask the head of the science department to show you the safety equipment and procedures in the chemistry laboratory. Ask the head of science about office equipment that might give off harmful fumes, or present other types of hazards.

INFORMATION TECHNOLOGY AND ADMINISTRATION SYSTEMS

Since the mid-1980s, **information technology** (IT) has developed at such a rate that it has been called a 'revolution'. The **information revolution** has brought great changes to administration systems as well as all other areas of business, for example, computer-aided design (CAD) and computer-aided manufacture (CAM).

IT is rapidly becoming subsumed into the majority of occupations. It is no longer simply a remote data processing tool or a piece of secretarial equipment. IT skills are no longer optional, they are essential to the successful completion of many jobs, including management. In most businesses, both large and small, there is a **personal computer (PC)** on almost every desk, from the chief executive down, through all levels of administration and operations. IT is as important as a pen or a tool box. However, it is not a substitute for the skills of the artisan and the imagination and creativity of managers.

PRESENT SITUATION

Almost every area of business is affected by IT: research, design, production, training, communication, and so on. In this element, our focus is on the use of IT in administration systems.

IT equipment in regular use in administration includes:

- ☺ mainframe computers;

- ☺ personal computers (PCs):

- ☺ laptop computers;

- ☺ PC workstations;

- ☺ laser printers

- ☺ fax and telex machines;

- ☺ client servers.

PCs are the most rapidly growing type of computer system. They are powerful, versatile machines which can be used by a person possessing little or no technical computer knowledge. They can support a number of input/output devices, including:

- ☺ keyboard;

- ☺ mouse and joystick;

- ☺ colour or black and white monitor screens;

- ☺ floppy disk drive;

- ☺ hard disk drive;

- ☺ CD-ROM;

- ☺ various types of colour or black and white printers, including high quality laser printers;

- ☺ sound output devices.

PCs are relatively cheap and can be purchased from a variety of sources, including stores like Boots, mail order outlets and office equipment suppliers. Shopping around can produce a wide range of prices. Software, on the other hand is relatively expensive particularly if it is tailor made for an organisation (see *Fig. 2.13*). However, software packages are available for most applications.

The most popular packages are:

- ✪ **spreadsheets;**

- ✪ **word processing;**

- ✪ **database management systems;**

- ✪ **desk top publishing;**

- ✪ **graphics;**

- ✪ **integrated packages for production, accounting, payroll, marketing and personnel;**

- ✪ **special purpose software for the doctors, dentists, accountants, solicitors, and so on;**

- ✪ **software for use in the home covering personal finances, inventory, home banking.**

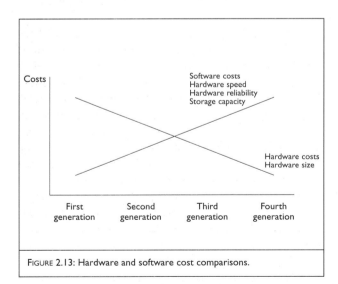

FIGURE 2.13: Hardware and software cost comparisons.

PCs can communicate over **local area networks (LANs)** or **wide area networks (WANs)**. This is a powerful facility that has resulted from the development of fibre optic digital networks over the telephone system. Through these networks all the electronic administration equipment can be interlinked. They can be connected by a single 'server' locally or, by multiple servers, to anywhere in the world.

For example, from the PC that this author is using to write this element, he is in daily contact with offices in England, Scotland, USA, Holland and Norway. All users of this network can call on a bank of twenty software systems and use them simultaneously without interfering with another user's data. These systems can be used by any number of individuals at the same time, or several users can collaborate and share data.

For example, three or four people, far apart, can be speaking through the telephone conferencing system as each of them is looking at the same data on a VDU screen on her or his desk. A one-hour telephone conference like this can save the group considerable time and expense in travelling to face-to-face meetings. Stress and fatigue are also reduced using these facilities.

ACTIVITY

1 Find out what computer-based administration systems are used in your school or college.

2 What software is used on them? Is the software a package or was it designed and tailored especially for the organisation?

3 If you can arrange it, ask one of the senior management team to explain the information that derives from the administration systems to assist with management decisions.

THE FUTURE

IT is developing very fast. It seems there is no end to its current progress. Whatever developments take place, IT is going to alter the way businesses are structured and the way they are administered. Tomorrow's environment will look nothing like today's.

VIRTUAL DREAM FOR SHOPPERS

Can you imagine shopping without the crowds, queues and over-heated fitting rooms? Well the shopaholic's dream is soon to become a reality for millions. The time is close when we will be able to buy the perfect outfit over the Internet, and anything from holidays to books through interactive television.

Electronic shopping is still in the early stages. But US analysts Killen and Associates predict that money transactions via the Internet will expand to more than £30bn by the year 2005.

There are around 30 million Internet users world-wide, one million of them in the UK, and usage is expected to grow at 10 per cent a month. So it is not surprising major retailers are eager to bring us all virtual shopping.

Last month, Barclays Bank opened its first electronic shopping centre with secure credit card facilities called BarclaySquare. Within just 24 hours of opening, 14,000 people had visited the centre.

There are only eight major retailers to choose from, but there are plans to expand in September.

'There is no space limit to how many retailers can join the centre,' says Christine Tucker, public relations officer for Barclays. 'But we want to keep it manageable. Shoppers will get lost if there are too many options on offer. BarclaySquare is there to supplement the shopping experience, not replace it. You can buy books from Blackwells, wines from Sainsbury's, gadgets from Innovations, and even book yourself a ticket to France via the Channel Tunnel.'

Double click on the Car Shop, and motor fans are provided with a range of information on new and used cars.

Click on the shop you wish to visit, browse, click next to the item you wish to purchase and take it to the checkout. At the virtual checkout you are given a total cost for the goods selected and you are required to key in your card number to ensure it is delivered to your home.

One question many users will ask is, can someone else hack in and use my credit card number? Barclays assures customers that credit cards are safe. Interactive Telephony Ltd joined forces with Barclays Merchant Services and Netscape to develop a method of making on-line transactions hacker proof. When a BarclaySquare shopper places an order by sending their credit card number down the line, that number is individually coded and can be deciphered only at the other end.

A more sophisticated system will need to be designed for direct money transfers but, so far, simple credit card transactions over the Internet are entirely secure.

CompuServe, the on-line information service, is the main competition for BarclaySquare, with its own electronic mall. It is not as far reaching as the Internet, but does have 100,000 UK subscribers, mainly young professionals on high salaries who are the perfect target for retailers.

At on-line W. H. Smith, you can buy books from a list of 250 bestsellers, at Virgin you can by CDs and videos and you can stop off at Dixons for a selection of electrical goods. On one day, shoppers clicked in at the rate of more than one per minute. CompuServe also hopes to persuade 15 retailers to join by the end of the year.

Daily Express, 9 June 1995

The article above predicts how retailing will change in the future. Although it refers to retailing and banking, all businesses could be affected. For example, some businesses have done away with the practice of everyone having her or his own desk. Instead, each person has a personal 'environment' in the corporate computer network. When they arrive at work in the morning, they have to find a vacant place, so long as there is a PC on the desk they can work as normal. This practice is known as **'hot desking'**.

Virtual reality is in its infancy, but its potential for business is very exciting. Christopher Barnatt, author of *Cyber-Business* predicts that there will be little need to assemble people for work, only for social interaction. Meetings will be held between people thousands of miles apart who, wearing their low-power laser scanners, can look around the 'room' and see everyone in their places, and interact as if it were a normal gathering. Nobody will go into 'the office'. The office will be wherever there is a PC linked to the corporate computer network.

The **Internet** can offer access to millions of people worldwide. A page on the World Wide Web can already reach ten million people. The Irish Tourist Board is already using it to sell holidays to a world-wide audience. A Scottish company is selling Scottish smoked salmon and Highland holidays through the Internet. The Bank of Scotland is on-line with its own page on the Web trying to find new customers. It believes that there is a potential market to be gathered from among the young computer literates. Visa is working on techniques which will make the transfer of money through the Web safe. Once this can be guaranteed, there is no reason why every type of business arrangement cannot be made via the Web.

The use of **'smart cards'** as a substitute for cash is also becoming a reality. A smart card is like a credit card with a chip in it. The card is put into a hole-in-the-wall bank terminal, where, after security protocols, a certain amount of money is 'down-loaded' from your bank account onto the card. You can then go shopping with the card and spend the money in any outlet with the right terminals. When all the 'money' on the card is spent, you can go back and replenish it – if, of course, there is money in your account. This system is being piloted in Swindon during the second half of 1995.

All new technology takes time to bed in and become accepted. It takes time for the average operations manager to appreciate the different ways in which IT can be exploited to improve business performance. New skills have to be learned by staff from the top to the bottom of every organisation. Old attitudes about how work should be done have to give way to new attitudes – and that can cause stress and worry.

But one thing is certain, IT is not going to go away; so it is best we become knowledgeable and skilful in its use.

ACTIVITY

Read the business section of any good newspaper. Cut out any reference to the ways new technology is affecting business organisations. Make a scrapbook which you can show to your colleagues.

IMPROVEMENTS IN SYSTEMS

Organisations are changing all the time. They are like evergreen plants; they sprout, grow, flower and, unless they are tended carefully, they will wither and die. If they are well looked after they will give pleasure for year after year.

Administration systems are changing too. They serve specific purposes in support of an organisation, and they must be flexible enough to change as the organisation changes. If they do not respond to their changing environment they will not serve the organisation and the organisation will certainly cease to exist in its present form.

Improvements in an administration system can be achieved by:

⊗ **constantly monitoring its performance against its objectives;**

⊗ **ensuring that the technology and equipment used to process the data are well maintained and up to date;**

⊗ **ensuring that the staff using the system are efficient and well trained;**

⊗ **ensuring that the managers using the information output from the system know what the output means and are trained in decision making;**

⊗ **taking care to see that procedures are efficient and modifying them to eliminate duplication;**

⊗ **introducing new procedures where appropriate.**

People who are not technical specialists in IT have to be trained in new skills. Unfortunately, we are not clear about what future training needs will be. Basic skills like using a keyboard efficiently, and knowing how to use applications, are unlikely to change. But where new concepts and methods are being developed, organisations will not get the full benefit unless people are trained to exploit them. That takes time. The consequence might be that opportunities to add value to performance are missed. The magnitude of time wasted by inefficient use of the technology is estimated to be 60 per cent of all real IT costs. This results in:

⊗ **increased staff costs;**

⊗ **a long timespan for the development and introduction of new applications;**

⊗ **slow implementation of change;**

⊗ **computer specialists spending up to 75 per cent of their time maintaining old applications rather than developing new ones;**

⊗ **heavy work load for computer specialists because of the need to maintain and develop systems, resulting in stress, fatigue, errors and constant staff turnover in this area of work.**

Hardware costs are reducing which encourages more companies to use more technology but the number of experts is not increasing at the same fast rate. Experience and training will correct all that, but both of these solutions take time. All new technology has shortcomings, but IT will continue its revolutionary progress in making business administration faster, more accurate, less costly and relevant to the precise needs of the users.

PORTFOLIO ASSIGNMENT

For this assignment, you need to arrange a meeting with a businessperson who is responsible for, or uses, a business administration system. She or he might be a person in your school or college, a relative or friend, a manager in a local firm that supports work experience, or someone in a firm that you contact at your own initiative. Before the meeting, prepare a list of questions you wish to ask about one administration system. The answers to your questions should give you information about:

- ✪ the purpose and objectives of the system;
- ✪ a description of the stages of the system;
- ✪ the forms used in the system;
- ✪ the input of data to the system;
- ✪ the output from the system for
  - (a) suppliers, customers, clients, etc.
  - (b) management decision making;
- ✪ the method used to process the data;
- ✪ the volume of data processed (for example, 5,000 invoices per year).

Prepare a business report which includes:

(a) some brief details of the business which operates the system, the way you contacted the business and how you gathered the information;

(b) a statement of the purpose of the system, a full description of the system accompanied by either a diagram or the actual forms used and an illustration of the data input to and the information output from the system;

(c) an analysis of the effectiveness of the system and its fitness for purpose, and an outline of the costs of the system.

Also explain, either verbally or by a presentation to your tutor, ways in which you might be able to improve the effectiveness of the system, and give your reasons for your findings.

Analyse communication in a business organisation

This element addresses some of the ways in which organisations communicate both internally and with the business world at large. Many businesses now operate in highly competitive global markets where the rapid, even immediate, response to changing trading opportunities and political situations can make the difference between profit and loss, survival and failure. It is essential that a business invests in, maintains, and regularly updates a reliable and effective communications system which makes use of efficient electronic processing and recognises the value of the human contribution.

THE NATURE OF COMMUNICATIONS

To communicate means to impart or convey information, meanings, instructions, requests and comment from one person to another using the media of speech, written text, sound, sign language, images, and even body language.

The act of communicating is arguably what human activity is all about. Nothing is achieved without communication, whether it is doing the shopping or building an aircraft. But the art of communicating is less straightforward; many problems, mistakes and disputes arise because the parties to a communication are confused by unclear instructions and misleading statements, or there is misinterpretation or a lack of understanding. In business, emphasis must be given to getting communication right.

Because we are now in the midst of an accelerating technological revolution, it is so easy to overlook the fact that even computer-generated documentation originates from people. The focus today is on the technology to the point that the computer is often blamed for errors when the true culprit is the operator who keys in the wrong information.

ESSENTIALS OF COMMUNICATIONS

Effective communication means, in simple terms, the sending of information in an appropriate form which the recipient is able to interpret exactly as the originator intends. Successful communication is reliant upon:

- ⊗ **timing;**

- ⊗ **clear thinking and expression;**

- ⊗ **attentive and careful reading, listening and interpreting.**

During the working day, individuals and companies are dealing with many different situations and personalities. There is the need to stick to company procedures and routines but it must be recognised that at times circumstances demand flexibility and initiative. Despite a dependence on technology, a business survives on its skills in handling people. Staff need to know when to be formal, persuasive, sympathetic, firm, and to appreciate when an informal, and more personal, approach will unlock a problem.

It is good advice to reflect on the purpose of any communication and the reasons behind it. Here is an example of a code of practice or set of basic rules:

- ⊗ **take the time to marshal thoughts about content, structure and objectives;**

- ⊗ **present ideas, requests, suggestions and instructions logically;**

- ⊗ **employ simple concise sentences;**

- ⊗ **use correct grammar;**

- ⊗ **avoid technical or legal jargon (except for specialists), outdated language, slang, and terms which some might find offensive;**

- ⊗ **adopt tone and style appropriate to the audience or recipient;**

- ⊗ **be courteous and exercise tact and sensitivity;**

⊗ **be impersonal;**

⊗ **use the most appropriate and effective medium;**

⊗ **encourage feedback.**

Some communications need to be complex and involved such as a technical description of switching gear. However, where it is practicable to do so, the code should be followed. When giving instructions, in either written or verbal form, it is advisable to adopt the 'kiss' approach – keep it simple, stupid!

ACTIVITY

Bring in an example of any form of communication which you find particularly difficult to understand. It might be a letter, instructions on how to complete a tax form or assemble a piece of furniture, a circular from the church or scouts, or a refund claim form issued by a store.

Form a small group with the other members of the class. Together, rewrite the offending items using the code of practice set out above. Present the new versions to the rest of the class or training session, indicating why the changes are thought necessary and how they improve the document.

METHODS OF COMMUNICATIONS

In analysing business communications, the first step is to consider the usual methods employed by an organisation. The following lists are extensive but they are not offered as complete or definitive. They indicate the variety of methods used by business and the range of options available.

Oral or verbal methods include:

⊗ **telephone;**

⊗ **audio-conferences;**

⊗ **conferences;**

⊗ **interviews;**

⊗ **committee meetings;**

⊗ **discussions;**

⊗ **instructions;**

⊗ **lectures;**

⊗ **role-play/business games;**

⊗ **team briefings;**

⊗ **management/staff consultative meetings.**

Written or textual forms include:

⊗ **letters;**

⊗ **memoranda;**

⊗ **reports;**

⊗ **balance sheets;**

⊗ **minutes;**

⊗ **summaries;**

⊗ **abstracts;**

⊗ **circulars;**

⊗ **notices;**

⊗ **in-house journals;**

⊗ **manuals;**

⊗ **charts and graphs;**

⊗ **statistical tables;**

⊗ **training documentation;**

- ☻ job descriptions;

- ☻ application forms;

- ☻ mission statements;

- ☻ policy statements;

- ☻ press releases;

- ☻ advertisements;

- ☻ packaging;

- ☻ catalogues;

- ☻ directories;

- ☻ computer print-outs.

Other methods include:

- ☻ video-conferences;

- ☻ radio/television;

- ☻ trade fairs;

- ☻ careers conventions;

- ☻ public meetings.

Material and information can be disseminated by using a variety of support equipment and services. These include:

- ☻ fax;

- ☻ electronic networks (E-mail);

- ☻ appropriate computer interface;

- ☻ telephone;

- ☻ radio pager;

- ☻ telex;

- ☻ telemessages (USA and UK only);

- ☻ postal/parcel services;

- ☻ courier services;

- ☻ the media.

In deciding on the method and means of communication, a business needs to consider the following factors:

- ☻ type of information;

- ☻ complexity and detail;

- ☻ accuracy;

- ☻ confidentiality/security;

- ☻ convenience;

- ☻ urgency;

- ☻ need for feedback and response;

- ☻ need to keep a record;

- ☻ cost;

- ☻ distance;

- ☻ number and location of people requiring the information;

- ☻ degree of formality/informality.

☀ ACTIVITY

Work in a small group and define or explain what is meant by these terms:

- ☻ audio-conferences;

- ☻ memoranda;

- ☻ in-house journals;

- ☻ job descriptions;

- ☻ mission statements.

Assemble a portfolio of at least ten examples of different kinds of genuine business communications. They need not all be good examples; attach to each item a note stating how effective or important you think it is.

OBJECTIVES OF COMMUNICATION

The lists of communication methods may seem overwhelming but they demonstrate the **variety**, **complexity** and **demands** of communications. Organisations expend much time and effort on the process of communicating. The primary objective is to pass on information so that business runs smoothly. However, communications can also play a significant part in motivating people, especially if management sees it as a process to involve rather than impose upon staff.

We now consider the differences between **internal** and **external communications**. Each activity may select from the same menu of methods and media, although their objectives are quite different. Internal communications relate to the transfer of information within an organisation; external communications deal with customers, suppliers, shareholders, etc.

The objectives of internal communications are to:

⊗ **initiate action;**

⊗ **encourage the flow of information and ideas;**

⊗ **give commands;**

⊗ **delegate;**

⊗ **report;**

⊗ **organise people;**

⊗ **encourage teamwork;**

⊗ **motivate;**

⊗ **influence attitudes;**

⊗ **encourage the work ethic;**

⊗ **encourage effective and efficient performance;**

⊗ **communicate results, goals and strategies.**

Consider your institution or employer. Identify and explain at least five methods of communication in regular use which you think help inform and motivate you, i.e. those communications which make you feel part of the organisation.

Internal and external communications operations may be separate because they focus on different objectives but they are in a sense related. If internal communications systems are weak, insecure and unprofessional then external communications are unlikely to be exemplary. One reflects the other. Companies with inefficient internal systems, which may demotivate staff, will find it difficult to create positive and effective external communications and build satisfactory relations with suppliers, clients and the general public.

The objectives of external communications are to:

⊗ **present the best image of the organisation to the world at large;**

⊗ **inspire confidence in the organisation;**

⊗ **encourage business.**

In supporting these main aims, a company may wish to communicate:

⊗ **the nature of its business or activities;**

⊗ **its record on industrial relations, equal opportunities, health and safety and the environment;**

⊗ **geographical areas of activity;**

- ✪ the response to and handling of complaints about products and services;

- ✪ the quality and content of the company's products and services.

The following groups will be among those targeted by external communications:

- ✪ pressure groups such as animal rights activists;

- ✪ local, national and European politicians;

- ✪ government at local, national and European levels;

- ✪ customers or clients;

- ✪ suppliers and other supporting companies;

- ✪ shareholders;

- ✪ the stock market;

- ✪ general public;

- ✪ the media.

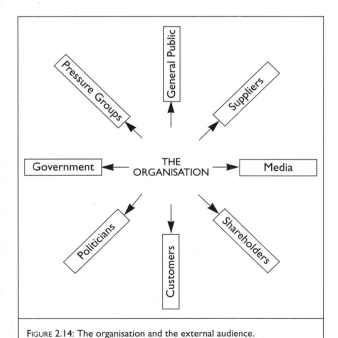

FIGURE 2.14: The organisation and the external audience.

ACTIVITY

Obtain two annual reports and balance sheets (from, for example, plcs, retail co-operatives and NHS Trusts) and examine how successful you think each is as a means of projecting the image and progress of the organisation to the world at large.

ACTIVITY

Your company wants to build a high-tech plant on a greenfield site. It is in an area of outstanding beauty and home to a variety of wildlife. The planning authority has no specific objections at this stage but public opinion is growing against your outline proposals. People believe that the area will be environmentally damaged. Your managing director thinks people should find something better to do, they should be grateful for the business coming into their area. If you are the public relations manager, explain how you would best communicate your company's plans and intentions to inform and reassure the general public.

COMMUNICATION FLOWS

The flow of information is dictated by the needs of management and by the structure of the organisation. Communications need to be co-ordinated and integrated so that the organisation can meet its corporate objectives. There are two official (or structural) and two unofficial (though often very productive) channels of communication. We shall consider each in turn.

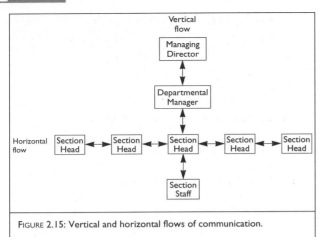

FIGURE 2.15: Vertical and horizontal flows of communication.

VERTICAL

The **vertical channel** reflects both the upward and downward flows of information. It is the route through which authority and responsibility are expressed. The downward flow is from superordinate to subordinate. It is used to:

- ⊗ **instruct;**

- ⊗ **delegate;**

- ⊗ **set targets;**

- ⊗ **inform;**

- ⊗ **persuade;**

- ⊗ **motivate.**

The downward flow, therefore, is the means to carry out the policies of the organisation. The upward flow is used to:

- ⊗ **convey feedback and response;**

- ⊗ **request approval for actions;**

- ⊗ **notify problems;**

- ⊗ **request solutions to problems;**

- ⊗ **report on target achievement;**

- ⊗ **report on human relations matters such as appraisals.**

HORIZONTAL OR LATERAL

Departments are organised to create areas of specialist activity such as personnel, sales, and research and development. But it must be understood that these departments or sections are part of, and must contribute, to the organisation as a whole. An activity initiated in one department may well have repercussions for several other departments and they will need to be appropriately informed so that they can respond accordingly. The **horizontal flow of information** occurs between departments (or other units of discrete or specialist activity) nominally at the level of supervision or management.

In an organisation which has a long chain of command and an authoritarian structure, the horizontal flow is often initiated by a vertical flow within a department. For example, a routine request for data by a junior clerk may be passed up through the structure to the departmental head who passes it to the head of another department who will then funnel the request down to the appropriate desk. Such a cumbersome structure is likely to encourage the informal flow.

INFORMAL

In order to operate effectively, an organisation is obliged to introduce procedures and practices covering the management of its internal structure. Despite clear procedures and well-defined vertical and horizontal information flows, it has to be recognised that some tasks would not get completed on time without people ignoring the **'chain of command'** and departmental demarcations. All organisations comprise people who have differing and sometimes conflicting personalities. Even in the best run organisations, the flow of information is likely to meet problems and mostly they are resolved by relying on **personal relationships**. So, for example, squash partners, even of unequal status, will co-operate 'unofficially' to achieve a result.

GRAPEVINE

A **grapevine** exists in every organisation and in terms of speed of information circulation it cannot be beaten. Its main feature, and disadvantage, is that it so often feeds upon rumour. Even if the substance is true (prospective redundancies for 5 per cent of sales staff), by the time the information has gone around the entire organisation, probably more than once, it will have become **exaggerated** and distorted (25 per cent of staff and closure of the southern area warehouse). But it is also true that the grapevine can pass on reliable information well in advance of any announcements. The usual sources are the 'invisible' employees, those who move about the organisation, in and out of offices and meetings largely unnoticed – tea ladies, cleaners and messengers. The grapevine can also be used quite deliberately by management to test the reaction of staff to suggested policies and proposals.

ACTIVITY

The senior management team are discussing the current position of the company over lunch in the boardroom. One manager says that the company would benefit from a 10 per cent reduction in staff and bonuses cut by half; business would grow by 5 per cent. After lunch, the personnel director is approached by a group of staff wondering if it is true that senior management has agreed to a large number of redundancies and pay cuts. Analyse this situation in a small group

1 **Identify possible sources of the rumour.**

2 **Discuss the methods the company might use to reassure staff.**

3 **Suggest ways that disinformation might be discouraged in the future.**

MANAGEMENT INFORMATION SYSTEMS (MIS)

Administration and communications systems are the processes through which a business generates, distributes, co-ordinates, monitors and completes its work. When all this activity is computerised, it is known collectively as the **management information system** (or MIS for short). It is not the name of any particular software package but rather a description of the overall function or purpose of the control systems within the organisation. A management information system is the collation of information and activities which assists or supports management. It may be used as a tool to support:

⊗ **decision-making;**

⊗ **directing the business;**

⊗ **forecasting;**

⊗ **monitoring performance;**

⊗ **progress chasing;**

⊗ **establishing goals and targets;**

⊗ **producing the balance sheet;**

⊗ **identifying loss making and/or slow moving lines;**

⊗ **calculating profitability;**

⊗ **VAT accounting;**

⊗ **order processing;**

⊗ **job costing.**

Information must be processed to meet both the overall needs of the organisation and the specific needs of the different levels of responsibility and authority within the organisational structure. Those doing unskilled routines may require a minimal information input, but those charged with formulating and/or advising on company policy will require access to all information sources.

As business becomes more complex, with the need to process the increasing amount of information in numerical, textual, sound and image forms, MIS will be regarded as an organisation's main strategic communications instrument.

THE EFFECTIVENESS OF COMMUNICATIONS

Communications tend to be taken for granted. Yet, so often, seemingly minor misinterpretations of data can create **problems** and **bottlenecks**. Stress is rightly placed on the effectiveness of communications. Without regular appraisal of, and improvement in, the methods and systems there is the threat of ineffective communications. Poor systems encourage:

⊗ **information hoarding;**

⊗ **lack of co-operation;**

⊗ **conflict and division;**

- feelings of demotivation, exclusion, insecurity, and even hostility;

- internal pressure groups;

- demarcation.

Insufficient attention to, and investment in, communications can divert a lot of energy away from meeting the organisation's stated mission objectives. Groups or individuals may develop their own agendas — a process which disrupts both the administration and working relationships. The importance of periodically reviewing the communications policy cannot be understated.

Simplicity has already been suggested as a feature of communicating, but as business and human activity gets complicated so too will communications. Even highly intelligent people are capable of mishearing or misapplying information. This can, for example, cause a situation of far-reaching legal consequences. So, effective communications play a vital role in determining business success.

It is therefore worth reiterating the characteristics of effective communications. Any communication needs to be:

- easily accessible;

- comprehensive;

- clear;

- informative;

- relevant to recipient's needs and circumstances;

- demand oriented;

- coherent;

- efficient;

- fast;

- flexible;

- delivered to the right addresses at the right time;

- unambiguous.

In addition, you need to pay attention to the following points:

- recipients must have confidence in the sender or originator;

- successful communications rely on the two-way process or exchange of information;

- all communications must reflect quality;

- the appropriate means of delivery must be employed.

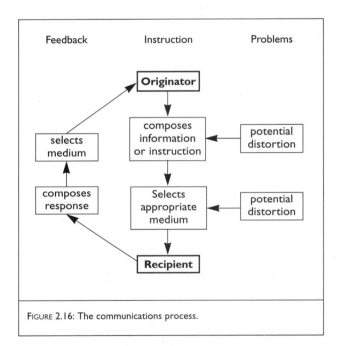

FIGURE 2.16: The communications process.

QUALITY

There is a saying 'garbage in, garbage out'. This means that careful attention must be paid to the processing of information. Computer systems do not, as a rule, make mistakes as the programs react logically to the given commands. Poor quality output reflects both poor quality input and poor information housekeeping. With global markets operating 24 hours a day, poor, ineffective or insecure communications may have formidable implications for an organisation. But, note, quality is just as imperative in verbal, handwritten and printed communications as it is in electronic forms. Limited vocabulary and a poor standard of English are as much barriers to effective communication as poor information.

MEETINGS

Many people claim to dislike meetings. Common complaints are that they go on too long, they do not focus on the issues, or they are badly run. But meetings can be important socialising and highly dynamic events. Notionally, they are expensive in terms of time and a budget-conscious manager may regard meetings as a lost opportunity, that is the participants could have achieved more by being at their desks. Equally, in the age of telecommunications you can argue that why bother to assemble in one location when there are audio/visual conferencing or electronic messaging facilities.

However, the disadvantages of electronic and remote media is the **lack of personal contact**. People are social animals and meetings create very different reactions to those experienced in remote conferencing. Meetings can identify the leaders and followers, the initiators and imitators, the proactive and the reactive. They can contribute to **team building** and provide **effective feedback**. For the people involved, attending a meeting means being 'in the know'. Ambitious staff use meetings to promote their own causes much more effectively than via memoranda, reports or teleconferencing.

Meetings should always be called for specific purposes. They should be positive and dynamic. Otherwise, they become affected by the 'sewing circle syndrome', with meetings being held on a regular basis almost solely for companionship.

ACTIVITY

List five advantages and five disadvantages to the individual of attending meetings.

CULTURE

Culture in this context means the attitudes and values of an organisation. Some companies have strict top-down organisational structures which may inhibit personal initiative and enterprise, and maintain long channels of communication. Others encourage a more open and democratic working climate supported by a recognition of individual contribution within a relatively flat structure. In this organisation, there is a short channel of communications between the boss and the functional teams and/or specialists. The culture of an organisation affects the working climate and it is likely to be reflected in the communications structure.

Information technology has brought considerable cultural change. As we have emphasised, organisations can now operate in a global business environment which demands they have fast, even immediate, and flexible responses. There is not the time to refer 'up the line' every single transaction or opportunity. Nor would it make business sense. IT-based companies, particularly those in international markets, encourage self-directing teams. These challenge any real (or supposed hierarchy) by imposing, by necessity, a flatter organisational structure.

The increasing use of IT has created more opportunity for employees to be directly involved in dealing with customers, suppliers, budgets and so on. In this sense, IT has empowered those people at the base of the organisational pyramid, who are now more frequently using and interpreting information and taking decisions.

DECENTRALISATION

In decentralised structures, the organisational pyramid is 'flattened' Long channels of communication are cut into short ones. Not only is the risk of distortion (through the rumour mill) reduced, but this process encourages employee involvement and participation. However, good intentions are not enough. If greater participation is to be achieved, companies need to introduce supporting policies.

One problem is to convince both 'them and us' (management and staff) that the organisation can work as a **people-centred operation**. It requires **open communication** and **feedback**. Organisations need to ensure that open consultation sessions are neither contrived nor starved of essential information.

There needs to be a culture of **information sharing**. This certainly reflects a cultural issue, and the availability of data at all times to all employees confirms the staff as partners and problem-solvers. Obviously, some access has to be restricted owing to the nature of the information (such as medical records, personnel files and patent applications).

New mechanisms may be needed for **problem solving**. Some organisations have set up **corrective action teams (CATs)**. The membership of a CAT is multi-functional. It assembles in order to tackle a particular problem and then disbands. This offers the opportunity for employees to participate in 'trouble-shooting'.

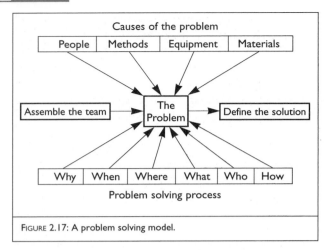

FIGURE 2.17: A problem solving model.

RESPONSES TO CHANGES IN COMMUNICATIONS

As organisations change, both management and staff can react positively or negatively to new developments. Some are regarded as **threats**, some as **opportunities**. Here, we look in turn at the negative and positive responses to changes in communications.

NEGATIVE RESPONSES

It is only to be expected that the prospect of change is accompanied by some feelings of concern. Where new electronic systems are being introduced, these preoccupations will centre on the following issues:

- ✪ **the compatibility of the equipment with external databases;**

- ✪ **security from eavesdropping and malicious damage;**

- ✪ **capability of the proposed configuration to be expanded;**

- ✪ **costs of installation, maintenance and operation;**

- ✪ **cost and extent of training.**

These may seem reasonable questions as no investment should be made without searching enquiry, but they become negative issues if people are subject to the 'FUD' factor (fear, uncertainty and doubt). If the technology appears to be 'too clever' then the major reaction, certainly among the senior and/or non-technical staff, is likely to be apprehension. If the power of the computerised system is stressed too strongly, staff (who may already feel insecure) will convince themselves that they cannot compete with the equipment, that somehow they are incapable. They may even try to resist the introduction of IT by creating obstacles or by proving the worth of a manual system or even by absenteeism. They may see computerisation as a threat to their employment.

Most jobs these days now demand keyboard skills. A senior manager dependent upon a secretary/PA and unused to a word processor, needs convincing of its value as a personal tool. If keyboard training is to be done by a relatively low-ranking employee, an exposure of ignorance may be feared. Other fears may be territorial: an electronic communications system may threaten a department's gatekeeper status. Some staff will not be comfortable with the notion of wider access to information.

POSITIVE RESPONSES

People at all levels in an organisation will be won over to the electronic revolution in their workplace once advantages have not only been demonstrated but experienced. Innovations like user-friendly software, immediate access to data and labour-saving procedures help win staff over. With the backing of employees, an organisation will be 'switched on' and technologically responsive. It should enjoy clear advantages, including:

- ✪ **improved speed of communication;**

- ✪ **improved access to communications;**

- ✪ **better working conditions;**

- ✪ **liberation of abilities;**

- ✪ **release from repetitive routines;**

- ✪ **opportunity for more responsibility;**

- ✪ **better control over job input;**

- ✪ **enjoyment of, and involvement in, problem solving;**

- ✪ **access to a much wider market and more business opportunities;**

- ✪ **connection to global telecommunications;**

- ✪ **opportunities for business creativity through electronic partnerships.**

IMPROVING COMMUNICATIONS

Having diagnosed a communications problem the next step is to suggest the remedy. In this section we consider several factors which, though insufficient in themselves, can when put together bring about a marked change in an organisation's culture. This can result in an improvement in **adaptability**, **loyalty**, **performance** and **communications**.

TRAINING

Training, itself, is not the remedy to organisational and communications problems. However, it is the means which can encourage people to be more receptive to change, to the needs of others and to the aims of the organisation. Some procedures can be taught directly, for example learning a new software package. But the process of developing team or participative work practices can only be developed effectively by using the trainees' own life skills and experiences – learning takes place through interaction with others.

The aims of training are to:

- ⊗ **reduce the perceived threat of technology;**

- ⊗ **learn to use the technology (and not be used by it);**

- ⊗ **adapt to the changing working environment;**

- ⊗ **encourage open communication and sharing of information;**

- ⊗ **remove the fear of staff participation;**

- ⊗ **remove the mystique of (but not the respect for) superordinate and specialist functions;**

- ⊗ **understand the organisation – its structure and mission;**

- ⊗ **encourage open mindedness and remove pre-packaged reactions;**

- ⊗ **stimulate team building;**

- ⊗ **develop social skills.**

ACTIVITY

Your company is experiencing problems with younger staff who cost a lot to train then often leave after less than a year. The personnel department is advising that recruitment should concentrate on the middle aged, particularly women who are returning to paid work after having children, because they will be more reliable. Your company is committed to IT and the new employees have no experience at all of computerised systems. Many even fear their own competence to cope with computers.

Work in a small group. Assemble an induction training programme designed to introduce new staff to information technology stressing its user-friendly nature and the ways in which office work is now organised. Design a one-day course and bear in mind it is an introduction to IT. Consider what is required from your own experience with IT.

TELECOMMUNICATIONS

The prefix **'tele'** comes from the Greek meaning far and it is in daily use in words such as telephone and television. It could be argued that all communication which is not face to face must be remote which therefore makes it telecommunication. However, the term tends to be used to denote the state-of-the-art electronic means of handling data (like sending high speed encoded messages from UK to Australia via satellite). The fax machine, which has become so indispensable to business, is clearly an example of telecommunications, and so is a terminal which accesses information from a datafile stored just 20 metres away.

The merger of computers and telecommunications has produced the multi-purpose workstation. This allows a wide range of activities that can be undertaken without the employee/user moving from the desk. A workstation offers:

⊗ **word processing;**

⊗ **numerical calculations;**

⊗ **transmission of messages;**

⊗ **storage and retrieval of information.**

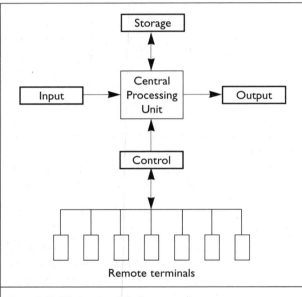

FIGURE 2.18: Workstations linked to a central computer.

A significant development in administrative work is that staff can have better control over their tasks and can enjoy more responsibility. Instead of completing just one function in a process, IT permits the integration of several functions allowing an individual to complete an entire task. The release from repetitive routines ought to be a motivating factor, staff should get more job satisfaction because they are making better use of their abilities.

ACTIVITY

Obtain the sales and publicity literature from at least two producers or retailers of hardware and software. Make notes on the range and prices of equipment and software

available. If you were to set up a small business, explain what electronic equipment you would buy and how you would expect to use it.

THE PAPERLESS ORGANISATION

Information technology has encouraged the idea of the **paperless organisation** in which all information and data is treated electronically. This should remove the need to maintain physical files full of letters, memoranda, reports, price lists and so on. All storage will be on disk and the transfer (i.e. the communication) of material will be entirely by computers 'talking' to each other.

This is not a futuristic notion. It is now possible to undertake a range of activities without being dependent on paper. However, paperless offices will not become commonplace until organisations are connected to the appropriate networks through compatible equipment. Current research, known as **OSI** or **open systems interconnection**, is looking at ways to allow any computer and network to combine with any other. Difficulties persist as there are so many different systems. The problem is one of **incompatibility**: without appropriate technology one system cannot directly talk to or communicate with another.

Curiously, the use of computerised systems has increased paper consumption and there has been a rapid growth in world-wide paper production. Even in 'high-tech' organisations, manual systems of administration still exist alongside the electronic.

COMMUNICATIONS BY COMPUTER

Communications by and between computers will be increasingly important in business. Already, there are a range of applications. These include:

⊗ **accessing electronic message networks using E-mail, for example;**

⊗ **accessing information which may be stored remotely from the head and subsidiary offices – for example, bank branches consulting customers' accounts held on a mainframe possibly hundreds of miles away;**

⊗ **accessing databanks of economic and trade information;**

- ⊗ an employee remotely updating company files when away from base;

- ⊗ teleworking – for example, a journalist can send in copy to a newspaper from a portable computer; many other specialists can work from home.

ACTIVITY

A Glasgow-based company employs a specialist who lives in Truro and works at home. List at least two advantages and two disadvantages of teleworking both for the individual and the company.

THE INTERNET

The **Internet** (short for international network of computers) originated in the USA in the 1970s when electronic links were formed between computers in the military and university sectors. Anyone with a computer, a modem, a telephone line and the appropriate software can access the Internet and communicate in **cyberspace**. By 1990, there were about two million users. The forecast is that there will be 200 million users by the end of this century. Internet really acts as a library – information can be put on-line on what are called 'sites' and users can access the datafiles.

ELECTRONIC DATA INTERCHANGE (EDI)

As speed and accuracy are essential to businesses, it is sensible to allow information (such as stock records, prices, finance proposals and manpower schedules) to be exchanged between organisations electronically. This reduces the scope for transmission errors. Information is exchanged by computers which can be linked using telephone lines. In order to make electronic data exchange work, **value-added data network services (VADS)** need to be added to the telecommunications network. These provide:

- ⊗ a means to enable terminals with differing speed of transmission rates (bits per second) to communicate;

- ⊗ a method of conversion (effectively a computer 'handshake') enabling connection and communication between incompatible terminals;

- ⊗ facilities for connection and message-routing;

- ⊗ facilities to enable messages to be stored for forwarding later;

- ⊗ gateways to other databases and services.

Many companies are dispersed not just within the UK but throughout Europe and the world. There is a need to maintain instantaneous communication. A telephone call is not sufficient to obtain the mass of information needed to make decisions. Electronic information exchange is the answer.

There is also a continuing need for efficiency. EDI allows the transfer of standard forms to be passed between computers of different organisations. This process bypasses postal services and fax, saves paper handling costs and makes better use of expensive time. EDI offers the prospect of a totally integrated business system when all organisations are linked via the **information superhighway**. Business can then be run with the minimum of personal contact.

EDI supports two new approaches to business administration: just-in-time methods and total customer responsiveness.

JUST IN TIME

Just in time (JIT) is a method of stock control in which little or no warehoused stock is kept within the company. Supplies are delivered 'just in time' for use. The advantages of just-in-time methods are:

- ⊗ fewer out of stock situations;

- ⊗ lower inventory costs;

- ⊗ reduction in staffing costs;

- ⊗ reduction in lead order times;

- ⊗ improved information about prices and product availability;

- ⊗ greater accuracy in ordering procedures.

TOTAL CUSTOMER RESPONSIVENESS

Electronic data interchange can stimulate the establishment of profitable partnerships between organisations in both vertical and horizontal directions. It offers firms the opportunity to develop more creative and effective ways of running business, generating new production and distribution systems for everything from handling raw materials to distributing finished goods and supplying commercial services. Some see this as the ultimate in organisational communications.

ELECTRONIC MESSAGING

The growth of electronic messaging systems has been encouraged by the rapid ownership of microcomputers for both personal and business use. There is, as a consequence, an ever increasing flow of information distributed in electronic form through a growing number of networks. There are many on-line systems that can be accessed over the telephone line. Some databases store financial and economic information, others will offer an up-to-the-minute news service.

A popular system is the **bulletin board**. This is the electronic equivalent of a noticeboard. It provides a convenient way of informing people about events, health and safety regulations, items for sale, etc. Many newspapers, especially the local free ones, have adopted the bulletin board approach; readers can send in their 'small ads' to dispose of a freezer or to offer gardening services. Electronic bulletin boards work on the same principle. They can contain advertisements and messages, and may stimulate the informal exchange of information.

The advantages of these messaging or E-mail systems are:

- ⊗ **messages can be read and dealt with when convenient to the recipient;**

- ⊗ **the sender knows that contact is assured as, unlike with telephones, there are no unavailable or engaged lines;**

- ⊗ **they are cheaper than telephone calls;**

- ⊗ **messages or letters can be sent to a number of subscribers at the same time;**

- ⊗ **messages of any length and complexity can be sent;**

- ⊗ **a printed record is available to both sender and recipient;**

- ⊗ **a system can be protected by a password so that messages and other information can only be accessed by those subscribing to it.**

ACTIVITY

Directorate General XXIII of the European Commission is responsible for enterprise policy. It has recently introduced two initiatives:

- ⊗ **an information network called Euro-Info Centres;**
- ⊗ **the Business Co-operation Network (BC-NET).**

Obtain details of these networks. Explain how they operate and list the benefits for subscribers.

MOBILE COMMUNICATIONS

It is estimated that by the year 2000 there will be forty million users of mobile communications in the European Union. This figure will double by 2010 and, by then, 50 per cent of business people will have mobile telephones. Including cellular telephones, paging and private mobile radio, the current market is less than twenty million.

SPECIAL NEEDS

Business information systems need to take into account the needs of the disabled. Among the disabled are employees at all levels, and clients. If the disabled are to be involved in the process of communication then some arrangements must be made to accommodate their various difficulties.

VISUALLY HANDICAPPED

If a person's sight is very limited or even non-existent, he or she has to rely upon other senses, particularly touch. Obviously, the hands are used extensively and the degree of sensitivity increases from the palm to the fingertips, which are very touch sensitive. Louis Braille, himself blind at three, invented a system of writing based on six raised dots in various groupings or configurations. These are felt by the fingertips, enabling a blind person to read. Expert braille readers can read at the rate of 150-200 words per minute. Braille documentation can be very expensive to produce but advances in technology have opened up access to information sources for blind people.

SPEECH SYNTHESISERS

For people who have lost the power to speak naturally, technology has provided a valuable aid in the electronic voice or speech synthesiser. Perhaps the most famous person to use this equipment is Professor Stephen Hawking of Cambridge University (author of *A Brief History of Time*) who suffers from a wasting disease and is confined to a wheelchair. The synthesiser enables him to continue his research and teaching. He has a computer attached to his wheelchair and by pressing a switch in his hand he can select words from a series of menus on the screen. His 'voice' is produced by the synthesiser, albeit in an American accent. The programme can store his dialogue and can also be controlled by a switch operated by head or eye movement.

THE INFORMATION SOCIETY

The information society refers to the way in which our daily business and personal lives are being transformed by the continuing IT revolution. As we have discussed, the business world is well served with electronic networks and, as more advances are made in computerisation, it will be possible to install a global telecommunications facility bringing computing services and within the reach of the general public.

The medium will be the **information superhighway**. This will carry simultaneous transmission of data, sound and images at very high speed and the user or recipient will be able to choose whether to read, watch or listen to it. Many applications are being considered. Below are just three of the potential benefits:

- ✪ **The creation of a world-wide electronic library will give every individual access to distance learning. This means that a UK student could gain a qualification by taking different modules selected from the world's universities.**

- ✪ **Business organisations will have access to expanded networks. These will, among other activities, encourage the exchange of commercial information, open up new market opportunities and enhance the efficiency of transnational payments.**

- ✪ **As the idea of the nine-to-five job becomes redundant, it is anticipated that there will be a growth in teleworking; more people will work from home or satellite offices and these locations can be anywhere in the world.**

PORTFOLIO ASSIGNMENT

You are to compile a report which investigates and analyses the internal and external communication in a business organisation.

First, select the organisation. This assignment demands much information and it is essential to choose a company or institution which is prepared to offer ready access to its communications systems. The approach must be flexible as it may be necessary to consult more than one organisation in order to collect all the evidence. If that is the case, make it clear in your report. You are advised to start with a familiar organisation such as your employer, school, college or local authority. Before you begin, consult the appropriate sections in the text and draw up your strategy.

The report needs to be divided into six sections which are identified by the specific tasks below.

1 Investigate three examples of internal and three external communication.

2 Analyse one example of internal and one external electronic communication. The examples should be considered in terms of their effectiveness in permitting access to information and encouraging interaction between people.

3 You should make two proposals for changes (or improvements) to the organisation's communications which should be justified in terms of their beneficial effects on the organisation.

4 Consider your proposals; explain two positive and two negative effects that the changes may bring about.

5 Define and explain the aims and objectives of your selected organisation.

6 Explain how this organisation uses communications to achieve its objectives.

Analyse information processing in a business organisation

INFORMATION PROCESSING

As we have discussed earlier in this unit, business is now approaching the **information age**. Organisations are investing large sums to produce systems capable of storing, retrieving, processing and communicating information. Information is now a very valuable commodity. Corporate information may be based on products, people or competitors. The effective use of information allows companies to understand their markets better and to become more efficient in supplying the products and services required. Information gives a firm a competitive edge over its rivals. Being able to predict future trends or accurately target potential customers will heavily influence the profitability of a company. The information sector is growing faster than the agricultural or manufacturing sectors, and is becoming ever more important in organisations.

In this section, we look at different types of information processing systems, analyse the effectiveness of information processing and explain the effects of the Data Protection Act on organisations and individuals.

THE PURPOSE OF INFORMATION PROCESSING

Information plays a key role in **decision making**. Companies need to respond rapidly to internal and external influences. Reports expressing changes in consumer preferences need feeding quickly through to the product design team. Changes in raw material costs must be evaluated by the finance department and acted upon. Before important company decisions are made, information will be gathered and processed to make sure that the correct actions are being taken.

It is important to **record historical information in an easily accessible form**. Companies store a range of historical information to assist in queries. This will include information for consumers, financial and personnel managers and shareholders. Information on customer

purchasing may be required to generate mailing lists, last year's sales figures may be needed to evaluate advertising campaigns, or personnel records may be needed to calculate sick pay. This information needs to be stored in a form which can be quickly retrieved, and presented in the manner required.

Systems that improve information processing allow employees to **work more efficiently**. A well-organised filing cabinet allows a clerk to reduce the time spent looking for records. Similarly (low cost) cash-point machines allow (relatively expensive) bank staff to concentrate on dealing with customer queries.

Word processor, desk top publishing and spreadsheet packages allow companies to improve their presentation of written materials. This provides **more effective communication** to customers, managers and employees. Increasingly, more sophisticated applications are being used to convey large amounts of information. As we have seen, organisations are now making use of E-mail, video conferencing and multimedia information centres, all as an aid to improving communication.

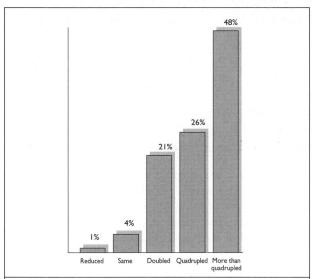

FIGURE 2.19: Growth of corporate information – executives report the extent to which information has grown over over the last decade. Source: Industrial Research Bureau for Reuters.

ACTIVITY

In groups of three or four, select one of the following areas of business activity:

- hotel reception;
- travel agent;
- supermarket;
- record store;
- market research;
- a large biscuit manufacturer's distribution centre;
- a brewing process;
- motor vehicle assembly line;
- newspaper publisher;
- fast-food store.

Identify and discuss those aspects of the activity where information technology is likely to have had a significant impact over the last five years in processing information.

THE PROCESS OF TRANSFERRING DATA INTO INFORMATION

Pages of unanalysed questionnaires are of little use to a company. They contain important data, but this data is not accessible. In its unprocessed form, it is difficult to extract useful and valuable information. The data – the small raw facts from which information comes – is, itself, of little or no value. To give it shape, the data must be transferred into information. Whether using manual or computer-based systems, this is the purpose of **information processing**. This process can be broken down into four main components:

- input;
- process;
- storage;
- output.

INPUT

The first stage is to input the data into a manual or computer-based system. In manual systems, this may be achieved by filling out a record card in ink. A computer system may mean using an optical character reader to enter data such as multiple choice answers on exam papers. There are many methods of inputting data into a computer. Input methods include keyboard, mouse and touch screen entry, as well as the more sophisticated methods such as **optical character recognition (OCR)** and **optical mark recognition (OMR)**. These last two methods are put to good effect in the Post Office to speed up the process of reading addresses on letters.

PROCESS

To transform data into information, it must be processed. This may involve collating all the pieces of data about one person, or making calculations on the figures entered. Processing involves changing the data so that it is ordered and related. The amount of processing depends upon the type of data being input and the required output. A printed train timetable contains information on arrival and departure times. Data has been inputted and processed so that passengers can quickly look up train times. This is of far greater value now it is ordered, it now contains information.

STORAGE

Though not strictly a part of processing, storing the information allows there to be a time difference between data being entered and information being supplied. A filing cabinet acts as a manual storage device. Similarly a hard disc drive achieves the same function within a computer system. By using a storage system, the data can be processed and then output many times at later dates.

OUTPUT

The purpose of processing information is to provide some form of output. This may be a summary table printed on a piece of paper, a figure displayed on a computer screen or a movement in a gauge. It is important that this output is in the form required by the user so that they can act upon it. With any system, there must always be some form of feedback to ensure that the information being produced is that which is required.

Once we have the information, we can analyse it and make informed decisions based upon it. After reading a train timetable, for example, the analysis may be that the train has already left, and the decision may be to go home.

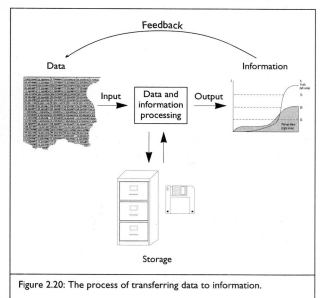

Figure 2.20: The process of transferring data to information.

WHO REQUIRES INFORMATION?

All departments, and all employees within departments, require information. This information may be anything from the price of an item in stock to the frequency of sales in summer compared to winter. However, although all departments may be accessing the same information, they are likely to be analysing it in different ways. The finance department will be more interested in costs and prices, whereas the marketing department may require product information on colours and sizes. It is important for all departments to have available the information they require in order to make important decisions.

At an **operational level**, organisations need to respond rapidly to daily issues. Shop assistants need to be able to give basic product information, determine which items are in stock and give prices for products. Secretaries may need to update customer details, produce well-presented letters and log incoming calls. All companies process information at an operational level each day. Without this information, many organisations would become inefficient in daily tasks.

In order to make longer-term decisions at a **strategic level**, managers and directors need to have important **performance indicators**. These may include current staff to capital ratios, sales forecasts or average sales by region. By analysing this information, senior managers and directors can make informed decisions on whether to build a new production plant, raise prices or increase capital expenditure. Without appropriate information,

they will be far less certain that decisions taken are in the best interest of the organisation.

THE REQUIREMENTS OF INFORMATION

Information is incredibly valuable to all companies. Without information, organisations will not be able to function to their full ability. Though information required may vary by department and by level of the operator within the department, there are several common requirements of all information.

Information must be **up to date**. A 1991 train timetable is worthless. The more up to date the information is, the more value it has. How recent the information needs to be depends on its use. Airline booking systems work in real-time, so their information must be accurate to the second. Here the information rapidly goes out of date. By comparison, a telephone directory system may only be updated yearly. Its value declines at a slower rate. In either case, the information must be current for its purpose.

Information must be **accurate**. Inaccurate information is worse than no information. For example, most people would prefer you told them that you do not know the time of the next train, rather than be given an incorrect time.

Information needs to be **relevant** to the task in hand. The same data may be required by different departments who each need to extract the information relevant to them. Irrelevant information requires more processing. It may be better to hold just important billing details on customers rather than to keep huge files containing information about past purchases, payment methods and other unrelated details. This way the information you require is much easier to access, and the cost of processing it will be reduced.

Only authorised personnel should have access to information. Valuable information should be **secure**. If a company has spent a considerable amount of money obtaining data, it would not wish it to be accidentally changed by an employee, nor would it wish its competitors to receive this information for free. Information should also be secure from fire, theft and (accidental and deliberate) damage.

Information is only of use if you can retrieve the information when and where you require it. It needs to be **readily available**. It is important that train timetables are available at the station, and that the ticket operators can look up train connections while you wait.

ACTIVITY

Choose a large bank or building society and assume that you have an account with it along with a cash-point card.

1 **List the banks and building societies which accept your card.**

2 **Identify the number of different cash-point machines, within your town or shopping centre, that accept your card.**

3 **Apart from being able to withdraw money, what other facilities are available from the machines?**

4 **Why do some cash machines have the facility to operate in several foreign languages?**

5 **Draw a flow diagram showing what happens to the information once money is withdrawn from a cash-point machine.**

6 **Give one reason why cash machines should give bank details which are:**

⊗ **up to date;**

⊗ **accurate;**

⊗ **relevant;**

⊗ **secure;**

⊗ **readily available.**

THE TYPES OF INFORMATION SYSTEMS

Information systems come in various flavours. At the basic level, you are processing information when you enter a new name in your address book or look up the telephone number of a relative. At the other end of the spectrum, there are systems which constantly monitor their environment and adapt under different circumstances. Submarine control systems take in direction headings and water pressure as inputs and feedback appropriate information to their operators. This ranges from position data through to engine tolerance levels. The submarine operators then make decisions using this information.

In any large organisation you will find text, number and graphic-based processing systems. There are a range of systems even in the most unlikely organisations. When you spend an evening in a disco or club, there are many information processing systems involved. Your leaflet will have been produced on a word processor or a graphics package. The takings at the bar will be processed by a spreadsheet, and there will even be a system to send output to the lights based on the music input received.

MANUAL SYSTEMS

Manual systems are operated by hand without the aid of a computer. For example, a filing clerk receives information, sorts it and places it in the correct file in a cabinet. Similarly, the clerk retrieves appropriate information from the cabinet. Though manual, this is still information processing. In any organisation there are considerable number of these types of systems. Manual systems tend to have the advantage of judgement and flexibility, however they are more prone to errors. We have all lost a friend's telephone number because we have not placed it correctly in our address book. A personal secretary to a managing director keeps the appointments diary; here, it is vital that an important client can fit into a tight schedule. A good personal assistant may be able to 'squeeze in' a brief meeting or delay a 'less important' appointment. A computer in a similar situation is unlikely to be able to make such allowances.

SINGLE-PURPOSE SYSTEMS

Single-purpose systems are introduced with the aim of targeting one function within an organisation. A computer is used to complete that function more efficiently. The single-purpose system only stores information relevant to that function or task. Examples of single-purpose systems are word processors, cash-point machines and loan repayment devices. In each of these examples, the system carries out one function only – to process words, to process account requests and to detail loan repayments to customers, respectively.

MULTI-PURPOSE SYSTEMS

Multi-purpose systems carry out a variety of functions. They may take data from many sources and process information for many different requirements. The system itself has more than one purpose. Unlike a cash-point machine which has the single purpose of processing individual account requests, the computer terminal inside the bank is able to process many different information requests. It is able to retrieve personal details about customers, list all accounts overdrawn and produce summaries showing the cash flow or transactions for that day. Different people within the organisation access the system, but for different purposes. The cashier uses it to verify your identity, while the manager uses it to analyse your banking record and make loan decisions based on this information. Multi-purpose systems are more expensive and require a greater amount of security than single-purpose systems.

MULTI-TASKING SYSTEMS

Multi-tasking systems carry out more than one task at the same time. If you can hold a conversation while you make a cup of tea, you are **multi-tasking**. You are carrying out two functions at the same time. If a computer must stop what it is doing to carry out a second task it will be multi-purpose. If, however, it can carry out a second request and continue with the first it is multi-tasking. An aircraft's navigation system must be multi-tasking. It must not stop monitoring the plane's altitude whenever the air temperature is required. It will carry out the two requests together. Many computer systems are now multi-tasking. Windows 95 and OS/2 Warp can both carry out more than one task at the same time. Using these systems, you can carry out a spell check while a spreadsheet is being recalculated in the background. Multi-tasking systems enable users to become much more efficient. Instead of waiting for a task to be completed they can carry on with another job. Their time is used much more efficiently.

ACTIVITY

Bainbridge & Anderson is a busy doctor's practice with over 6,000 patients. Currently every patient has their own record card and associated file. Each of these is stored in one of five filing cabinets. At the surgery there is one full-time and one part-time receptionist. Each doctor has an appointment book as well as a list of clients requiring home visits.

1 **What would be the advantages of computerising the information systems within the surgery to:**
   (a) the doctor;
   (b) the patients;
   (c) the receptionist;
   (d) the overall operation of the surgery.

2 **How would a multi-purpose system enable the doctors and receptionist to work more efficiently?**

THE EFFECTIVENESS OF INFORMATION PROCESSING

The process of transferring data into information is a costly one. It may involve questionnaires, manual data entry into a computer system and expensive data processing before it is of value to a company. It is important that the **benefits** of the information outweigh the **costs** involved in acquiring and processing it. There are many ways of processing the same information. Organisations must choose the most effective system, in terms of **speed**, **value for money**, **reliability** and **security**. Some video rental stores take your details and manually enter them onto a record card. Your record is updated by hand each time you rent a video. Other stores enter your details into a computer database that effectively mimics the manual process. The newer, and more sophisticated, information systems link up to other services. With these stores, your post code is sufficient to provide your address for the system. If you return a video late, the system automatically bills you. The system also monitors the frequency of your visits and possibly the types of videos you rent. All of these different systems achieve the same goal of supporting a video rental business. Some methods are more appropriate than others at processing the same information. Organisations need to consider carefully several factors before choosing the most effective method for processing data.

FITNESS FOR PURPOSE

The first factor is whether the method can deliver the required information within given **specifications**. A new travel agency would set certain targets such as accuracy of information, time limits for enquiries and levels of detail required. A manual system is very unlikely to meet these specifications.

The second factor is whether the information output from the system is in a **usable form**. A system analysing questionnaires must produce information which directly helps decision making. A company conducting market research on beauty products needs the output in a form which provides objective information such as the price consumers are willing to pay or the number of hair products purchased in one month.

Systems which provide information which can be interpreted in several ways are of far less value. If a system is processing results from a fruit survey, you might draw from this that a hair care product should have the same smell as the most popular fruit. This would be one subjective interpretation. Another might be that sweet, sickly smells are more popular to eat, but sharp, clean smells are preferable for a shampoo. To be fit for the purpose required, systems are usually expected to give **objective information**: if information remains open to subjective interpretations, a company is left with a series of unanswered questions requiring further data processing or more research.

EFFICIENCY

Typically, a computer can work many times faster than a human being. Computers like repetitive tasks, require no breaks and are totally accurate. Provided you can feed the information into a computer as fast as it can process it, a computer can be very efficient. After being 'taught' how to sort a list, or group data, it is able to repeat this task indefinitely. The efficiency of a system may be measured by the quantity of facts and figures retrieved in a time period or by the time it takes to retrieve a piece of information. With either measure, the efficiency must also take into account the cost of such processing as well as how quickly a new user can operate such a system.

Doonesbury

BY GARRY TRUDEAU

INFORMATION RETENTION

Where a human may forget a piece of information, a computer will not. It is able to store innumerable pieces of information and still be able to access the relevant data. However, a computer may become corrupt or lose data because of a **computer virus**. A filing cabinet has no such drawback. Organisations must take into account the quantity of data and the length of time that it will be stored.

SECURITY

Just as an office can be broken in to, so can a computer system. Many personal computers are not adequately protected from thieves or from intruders wishing to gain information. It is important that, whatever system is used, the information held is evaluated and appropriate security measures are taken to ensure that it is kept safe. With manual systems, fireproof safes should be used and locks placed on doors. With computerised systems, virus and password protection should be in place.

COST

A manual system is inexpensive to set up. It has fairly constant running costs. The cost of setting up a manual telephone directory system is likely to be approximately one day's training and the hourly rate for the operator

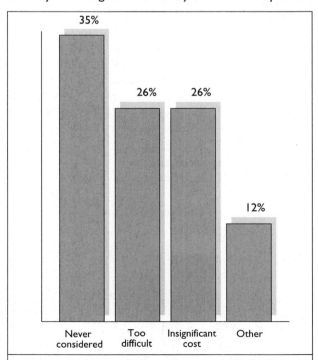

Figure 2.21: Why companies do not track the costs of computer-based information systems.
Source: Industrial Research Bureau for Reuters.

from that point on. Being a manual system, the member of staff is only able to deal with a limited number of enquiries. If the volume of enquiries increases, then another operator will need to be placed on call, generating similar costs. For small volumes of processing, manual systems offer a flexible, cheap solution.

For larger quantities of processing, a computer may be more cost effective. There is a cost involved in starting up computer systems, of which staff training can be a high proportion. For this reason, increased quantities of data must be processed before a computer system becomes economical. A computer system, however, is likely to be equally happy handling ten requests as it is handling a hundred. Within most organisations, there is a point at which a computer becomes more cost effective than a human at the same task. Depending on the requirements, single-purpose, multi-purpose or multi-tasking systems may be used, but the cost implications associated with each should be taken into account.

THE EFFECTS ON INDIVIDUALS AND BUSINESSES

The rapid progress in information processing has affected businesses and individuals alike. There has been a change in the structure of many countries' economies and output. Historically, the dependence on agriculture was followed by the dominance of industrial output. Increasingly, it is the service and information sector which is growing. Whole businesses have sprung up based on the sale of accurate, relevant information.

ORGANISATIONS

The information revolution has given organisations access to information which is more detailed, reliable and accurate than previously available. Complex management information systems allow well-informed decisions to be made, based on comprehensive and up-to-date information. Systems are available which allow tasks to be performed in a fraction of the time that it previously took, with total accuracy and near-perfect reliability. Organisations are adopting a variety of these systems at all levels to improve efficiency and maintain a competitive advantage.

As well as allowing organisations to use this information for their own purposes, companies can manipulate information, and sell it on to other companies. If you enter a competition for a hi-fi system, you might later receive a string of other 'offers' ranging from compact discs to holidays. Once an organisation has information on a target group of customers, it becomes valuable to other companies with a similar market. The speed of computers and the ease with which information can be manipulated has led to a growth in **information sale and exchange**.

In order to take advantage of these improvements, organisations have had to invest in sophisticated equipment and communication lines. In many cases, the structure of the organisation has changed to reflect the increased importance of information. Where supermarkets previously had a high percentage of staff pricing and ordering stock, information systems now automatically take care of this. This equipment, and the training which much accompany it, needs to be regularly updated to ensure that the competitive edge remains.

As companies invest in new technology, they must also meet the associated costs. Old and new systems may be incompatible. Data must be converted across, printers re-configured, and new communications cables laid. Staff will require training to use the new system effectively and security measures must be put in place to prevent the loss or theft of data. Often newer, more sophisticated, systems are introduced into competing companies only one year after the installation of the previous system. Organisations must then decide whether to follow suit or wait for the next generation of information developments.

INDIVIDUALS

The skills required by employers have changed over time because of the changing structure of the economy. Previously, workers may have based an entire career on a single skill or trade. They are now expected to have a **broad range of skills and experiences**. The increased use of computers has led to many repetitive jobs being undertaken by machines, while employees now deal more with the data entering and leaving these systems. As a result, working conditions have improved and employment opportunities for disabled or part-time workers have risen. Many jobs are office based, requiring less physical effort. As systems continue to develop, so employees will be required to adapt quickly. This has large training implications. The opportunities for computer operators, and those with associated skills, have increased, and this is likely to continue as the value of information increases. The main negative effect of these developments is the increase in computer-associated health problems. **Repetitive strain injury (RSI)** from keyboards, headache and eye strain from monitors, as well as a general rise in stress levels from equipment malfunctions, have all affected employees' health.

DATA TRANSFERS MAKE THE NEWS

Associated Newspapers has just completed one of the UK's most ambitious electronic data transfer networks, processing newspaper sales and returns information from more than 55,000 retailers across the country.

The company claims that the system, which was completed last month, has already paid for itself twice over since last July, when the first information started flowing across it.

Associated is the first company to make full use of the national retail information network set up by Newpet, an electronic trade committee made up of newspaper and magazine publishers and their wholesalers. Under the system each wholesaler uploads information to each publisher detailing the number of papers sold and the number returned from each retailer it supplies.

Associated is processing this information and feeding its regional sales reps data on the retailers in their areas.

'The aim is to reduce returns and increase the availability of papers,' said Michael Jones, Associated's IT director. 'We have already achieved a 200 per cent payback in one year.'

The information is stored at Associated Newspapers in a database running on Digital Alpha servers. The largest wholesalers send information direct to the company, while smaller ones use value added networks or simply dial in over the public phone system. Sales reps can dial into the database from their laptops to download the latest figures.

Jones said the system, which has allocated a unique identifying number to every newsagent in the country, could be expanded beyond newspapers. 'Other groups are already applying to use the numbers,' he said, 'including confectionery forms.'

Computer Weekly, 8 June 1995

ACTIVITY

Read the article on data transfers above. Then answer the following questions.

I   **Before the new system was introduced, what information might newspaper retailers send to Associated Newspapers?**

2   **How might the introduction of the system have 'paid for itself twice over since last July'?**

3   **What are some of the hidden costs in installing such a system?**

4   **How could the system develop in the next five years?**

THE DATA PROTECTION ACT 1984

Systems which process data have become increasingly sophisticated over time. Analysing and transferring data has become much more cost effective. The **Data Protection Act** was introduced with the aim of preventing people abusing personal data held on computers. Any organisation, whether in the public or private sector, must register details of data held on individuals with the **Data Protection Registrar (DPR)** and adhere to the eight principles of the Act. Some information is excluded under the legislation, including data held by sports clubs and data held by individuals for personal use. These few exceptions aside, all organisations holding personal data on computer must pay the £75 registration fee and obey the principles. Organisations failing to comply face a maximum fine of £5,000.

THE EIGHT PRINCIPLES OF THE DATA PROTECTION ACT

THE DATA SHOULD BE OBTAINED AND PROCESSED FAIRLY AND LAWFULLY

It is important that a person should know that the information they are giving is being held on computer. There should be no deception involved and they should be made aware of the reason for the data being held. It would be unfair (and unlawful) to obtain personal information from an unregistered source.

THE DATA SHOULD BE HELD ONLY FOR SPECIFIED PURPOSES

Data can only be held for purposes which are registered with the Registrar. If for example, the doctors' practice

Bainbridge & Anderson wishes to hold data relating to its employees for accounting and personnel reasons, it must register this use.

THE DATA SHOULD NOT BE USED OR GIVEN FOR OTHER PURPOSES

This principle focuses on not using the data outside of the purpose for which it has been registered. This includes giving the data to third parties. Bainbridge & Anderson would not legally be allowed to pass employees' details to an insurance firm as this purpose was not registered.

THE DATA HELD MUST BE RELEVANT AND NOT EXCESSIVE

It is important that a company holding computerised information does not record more information than is strictly required for its intended purpose. Similarly, they should not hold irrelevant information. It would be legal for a garage to hold customer information regarding recent repairs and the make and model of the car. They would have no reason to include the age of customers or their credit card number in customer files. This would be illegal as the information is both irrelevant and excessive for the purpose of keeping customer purchase records.

THE DATA SHOULD BE ACCURATE AND (WHERE NECESSARY) UP TO DATE

Inaccurate information is irrelevant. More important to the individual is that it may be harmful. An individual's ability to borrow money for a car or holiday is likely to be based on his or her credit rating. If this information is not correct, then credit requests will be refused, or inappropriate limits will be set.

THE DATA SHOULD NOT BE KEPT LONGER THAN IS NECESSARY

If there is no need to keep data after a certain period, the organisation should destroy that information. It would not be necessary to keep personal information on employees after they have left the organisation. These records should be destroyed soon after employees leave.

INDIVIDUALS ARE ALLOWED TO ACCESS AND (WHERE APPROPRIATE) CORRECT DATA HELD ON THEM

The Data Protection Act gives provision for any member of the public to find out what information is held on computer about them. An organisation is required to give this information within forty days, though may charge a small administration fee (of up to £10). The individual is then provided with a printout of all the information. If information is inaccurate, the individual can request that the data be changed, or where appropriate deleted.

SECURITY MEASURES MUST BE TAKEN TO PREVENT UNAUTHORISED ACCESS TO THE INFORMATION

Organisations must take precautions to prevent unauthorised access to personal information. This will involve physical barriers as well as digital methods. Information, and the computers on which they are stored, should be in a locked room. Any back-ups, discs or printouts of the data should also be locked away. If the information is available on a network of machines, adequate password protection should be in place, so that only authorised personnel may gain access to the information.

'A London-based design company, worried about the dangers of fire, stored all of its valuable information archives in a fireproof safe. The fire never came but thieves did and the only item they stole was the safe.'
The Times, 3 March 1995

ACTIVITY

In groups of three or four, discuss why computers have made it necessary to have a Data Protection Act. During the discussion, consider the following issues:

- **speed of processing;**

- **cross-referencing;**

- ✪ analysis tools;

- ✪ cost of replicating data.

Discuss why some organisations may still not have registered under the Act, despite it being on the statute books for more than ten years.

THE IMPLICATIONS OF THE DATA PROTECTION ACT

FOR THE INDIVIDUAL
The Data Protection Act has given individuals the ability to find out what information is being stored on them by any organisation. It gives them the ability to correct inaccurate information and to remove their details from computer systems where the information is no longer required or where the company does not have the right to hold such information. Under the Data Protection Act, an individual's information is secure from being used for purposes not registered with the Data Protection Registrar.

FOR ORGANISATIONS
The Data Protection Act has forced organisations to look much more closely at the information they are storing on computers. Previously, there was no structure or procedure; now, companies can no longer keep unnecessary computer files about individuals. They must manage this information responsibly. Records must be kept up to date, must be accurate and security devices must be in place to prevent unauthorised access. Although this has ensured that the information a company holds is more valuable, it has placed a large financial burden upon business. It is not uncommon for an organisation to have a data protection officer to monitor compliance with the Act and to deal with requests from individuals. If an organisation fails to register data, or does not comply with any of the eight principles, it can be fined a maximum of £5,000.

LATEST DEVELOPMENTS IN DATA PROCESSING

The methods used to process data are constantly developing. More sophisticated analytical tools, along with increased computing power are providing organisations with information which allows them to focus their activities more effectively.

DATA WAREHOUSING AND DATA MINING
Many organisations now hold data from a wide variety of sources. By creating **data warehouses** of information, they can react far more easily to new patterns and can use analytical tools to provide more information than just past sales. For example, while existing records may only be able to provide details of sales of ice cream in the previous year, the data warehousing approach would be able to put this information together with weather forecasts, consumer preferences and any other information available to the organisation. This warehouse of information can then be analysed to provide predictions. These analytical tools can sift through the data effectively. They are more complicated and, therefore, expensive but the results can be quite astounding. For example, using **data mining techniques** to find patterns might show a company that sales of fast food are linked to sales of video rentals. This may lead to joint marketing campaigns targeting this group of people.

GROUPWARE
Packages are being developed to allow employees to share information more easily within their work group. This includes documents, figures, diaries and databases. The team may be spread throughout a building, or across several countries. The software allows these individuals to work together on the same project, as if they are sharing the same machine. All of the group are able to work on their individual areas, but can then easily tie in their work with that of their colleagues. This flow of information between users provides each with a clearer view of how their input fits in with the whole team.

THE INTERNET AND DATA PROCESSING
One of the fastest growing areas of information is the **Internet**. This interconnection of thousands of computers unleashes quantities of data which are almost limitless. The data on the network covers everything from products and services through to educational establishments and

even transcripts of court hearings. It is now possible to call up the weather in any country, receive copies of today's newspaper articles as well as search for specific information.

The data on this network, though freely available, is often in a very raw state. Data about drinking habits may be scattered across continents, and within these continents may be found on hundreds of different computers. In this state, the data may be of no use to Coca-Cola or Cadbury Schweppes. For organisations to fully utilise the available data, very powerful information processing and data retrieval engines need to be created. These will collect, process, and report on relevant data from around the world. Once this information source is tapped, organisations will be even better placed to make global decisions.

PORTFOLIO ASSIGNMENT

1 Arrange to visit a local organisation with a view to investigating the information processing taking place within one particular aspect of the organisation such as finance, marketing or production.

2 Find out what systems there are for numbers, text and graphics within this area and look at the efficiency of these systems.

3 Produce a brief report which explains the information processing taking place. Ensure your report includes the following:
   (a) how the information is received;
   (b) how it is entered into the system;
   (c) what format the information is in;
   (d) what information is retrieved from the system;
   (e) who the information is given to;
   (f) what actions are taken after this person receives the information.

4 How could any of the systems be improved upon?

5 Outline how the organisation has responded to the Data Protection Act.

6 Explain the relevance of the Act to the area you have investigated.

Index